Graham Willis was born in 1961 and lives in London with his wife, Sheila, and their son, Kylam. He has worked in the removals and storage business for 30 years which was originally started by his family in 1930. This is his first book and is a tribute to all the family and friends who have supported him through the years, especially his mum and dad.

To Don Willis, Grandma Willis, Kylam Willis, Trevor, Matthew, John, Dave, Rob, Mark, Jerry, Nigel, Sean, Jonathan, Tony, Henry, Vince, Jason, Alan, Daniel, Michael, Richard, Conor and Ryan who have worked hard with me for the last 30 years to create a lifetime of memories.

Graham Willis

MEMOIRS OF A REMOVAL MAN

AUSTIN MACAULEY PUBLISHERS™

LONDON • CAMBRIDGE • NEW YORK • SHARJAH

A CIP catalogue record for this title is available from the British Library.

ISBN 9781528975148 (Paperback)
ISBN 9781528976305 (ePub e-book)

www.austinmacauley.com

First Published (2021)
Austin Macauley Publishers Ltd
25 Canada Square
Canary Wharf
London
E14 5LQ

Thank you to my wife, Sheila, for being by my side for 26 years.

Introduction

Moving house has been likened to death and divorce in the list of most stressful experiences; when I joined the family removals business at the age of 29, I entered this world of organised chaos myself, witnessing heart-warming and sometimes traumatic scenes on a daily basis.

I had grown up helping out with removals from an early age in the 1970s when it was still acceptable for my brother and I to ride home from journeys waving out the back of the removal truck to passers-by and other motorists.

Having kept a diary for 30 years, as well as delving in to the company archives, I am able to give an insight in to the experiences of moving home, not always seen but that will be familiar to many. Most are personal experiences but a few stories have been related to me by other removal men over a cup of tea in the local café; like the London company.

whose men had to smuggle the clients' mistress out of the bedroom on arrival at the job as his wife had arrived earlier than expected. They used a wardrobe container, which is normally for transporting clothes, to carry her down the stairs and out of the house to safety.

So here follow my diaries from those years, some good and some bad times but always interesting.

Before My Time

Monday, 12ᵗʰ February 1940

Load the contents of a house in Northwood and drive to
Torquay, Devon; during the war everything was blacked out
with masks on the headlamps and no streetlights making
driving long distances extremely difficult.

There were no signposts as these had all been taken down,
the fog was so thick on the journey home that when my
granddad eventually turned in to his driveway, the cars behind
followed him. Cost of removal: £16. 10 shillings.

Monday, 16ᵗʰ December 1940 to Tuesday, 24ᵗʰ December 1940

8am to 6.30 pm: meet the post office train with a removal
van at Harrow & Wealdstone station; collect the Christmas
mail and deliver to the local sorting office. Daily cost of
removal: £4. 9 shillings. 3d.

Friday, 4ᵗʰ August 1961

Collect scouts from local scout hut in the removal van and
drive to a campsite in Wimborne, Dorset. When my dad
opened the back of the van on arrival, he discovered the scouts

had been practising their knots using the webbing hanging from the sides; he then refused to allow the scouts to leave the van until they had undone all the knots!

Friday, 25th November 1966

Dad and his younger brother Doug are cleaning their vehicles in the driveway of Pinner Road, North Harrow which my grandmother has rented since 1930; it is the house where they run the business from. After using a variety of cleaning materials including paint thinner, they decide to pour them down the drive and hide the evidence from my gran by setting light to it. Grandma Willis was stopped by her neighbour while at the local shops.

'Your boys have set fire to the road!' she exclaimed. The flames had spread down the driveway along the gutter before disappearing down a drain; they were both in the dog house on her return.

1991 to 1994

Monday, 20ᵗʰ May 1991

The first day of working with my dad; loading a house in Eastcote for removal to Northampton. Whilst lifting the mattress from the bed, I discovered £1000 in cash underneath that our customer had hidden and forgotten about; she was very grateful to have it returned.

We arrived at the new house on an unusually hot day in May to find we were unable to start unloading as there was a delay with the money being transferred between solicitors, so the keys to the property would not be released.

This would become a familiar theme throughout my 30-year career and a constant source of frustration to all involved; except of course the solicitors who just extended their lunch and added it to the bill! Whilst waiting in the cab of the truck, we were kept amused by the neighbouring property having a new driveway laid. The hot weather meant the cement was setting too quickly, and the men laying the drive were desperately running about trying to smooth and shape it before disaster struck. Glad we are not the only ones having a difficult day.

Tuesday, 20th August 1991

Left Harrow early at 6.30am having loaded the truck yesterday for a journey to Worcester. This is our favourite route as it involves driving through the Cotswolds, Cheltenham and then the Malvern Hills; I am driving the Bedford truck on L-plates as have yet to take my HGV test and share the driving with my dad. He knows the best routes and also the best transport cafés to stop on the way; unfortunately, these are already dying out, but there are still a few left offering a fantastic fried breakfast for a reasonable price We have a portable radio in the cab and there is a news announcement saying,

Russian president, Mikhail Gorbachev, has been arrested during an attempted coup by communist party leaders. This is a world away from the beautiful country roads we are travelling along; it is strange how you can remember where you were when important world news events occur.

Saturday, 24th August 1991

Went to our warehouse in Pinner to load furniture and T chests (were not using cardboard boxes yet) for delivery to Wealdstone. This warehouse my dad has used for over 20 years, and consists of 18th century barns which would eventually become 21st century barn conversions. However, at this time they are very much farmhouse barns which although providing suitable storage, were at the mercy of barn rodents.

The customer's belongings had been in storage for 3 months and all appeared well when loading on to the truck. On arrival at the new house, my colleague, Trevor, carried a

T chest in to the living room from which, suddenly, a family of mice appeared who had been nesting in the paper wrapped around household china. He started shouting for my dad to come quickly and we both ran in to the room to see little mice hopping out of the T chest.

Luckily, the lady of the house was in another room at the time and we were able to stuff the mice back in the T chest and run out of the house before anyone started screaming. I am still not sure if we caught all the mice or if the owners gained a new pet as a housewarming present.

Wednesday, 18th September 1991

The first self-storage company in the area has opened in Wembley, so we decide to try their warehouse as an alternative to our barn. After loading from a house in South Harrow, we drive to Wembley and start unloading in to the metal room of the self-storage unit. This involves using their industrial lift as our room is on the first floor; unfortunately, I am in the lift with my dad when there is a shudder and the lift stops a few feet off the ground floor. As we are unable to open the doors and climb out, we have a long wait for the fire brigade to come and winch the lift back down. We never had this trouble in the barn!

Monday, 14th October 1991

Dave, a good friend of mine, works in the civil service and has done so most of his life; his department in Kensington is in charge of arranging the logistics for a government inquiry taking place in Chichester. He needs some archive files, chairs and filing cabinets delivered to the conference room of a hotel in Chichester; a colleague of ours has his own small van, which is more suitable to gain access to both addresses, so Mark and I set off in the morning for Kensington.

The inquiry is to last two weeks when we will be tasked with the job of collecting all the files etc. and returning them from Chichester to London. The judge overseeing proceedings is charging £1000 per day, so our removal cost is a drop in the ocean, but it does seem a waste of a lot of tax payers' money.

Tuesday, 5th November to Friday, 8th November 1991

I have booked an HGV four-day course of intensive training to prepare for a driving test next week. There is myself and a Harrow Council employee taking lessons and practising our driving together with the driving instructor who looks like he could use less lunch breaks and more exercise. As part of our driving practice, he gets us to do a variety of stops for him during the day which include his photography studio where there are models in various degrees of undress. Perhaps this is all part of the HGV driving test!

Monday, 11th November 1991

HGV driving test today at 10.30am, so I arrive at the test centre in Hayes for 10am and watch other drivers reversing in to coned areas as part of their test as well as performing emergency stops before going out on the road. 'Don't worry,' says my instructor, 'you'll be fine so long as you don't get the Scottish examiner.' I wait in the reception area until the examiner appears, and although he is not wearing a kilt, I am pretty sure I have drawn the short straw with Mr McKay!

I walk to my truck feeling a little nervous while he stands alongside to watch me reverse in to the coned off area. While I had been waiting in reception, an identical truck to mine had also parked, and I got in to the wrong cab only then realising that there was an articulated trailer attached to this one.

After making a hasty red-faced exit, I got in to the right cab and started to reverse: having to stop the rear of the truck the correct distance from the cones.

There were other people watching as I had been, and once they had stopped laughing at my misfortune with the wrong cab, one of them helpfully gave a discreet thumbs up when the truck was positioned correctly.

Out on the road all went well and I returned an hour later with a pass and a huge smile on my face.

Friday, 15th November 1991

We are moving a local estate agent today in to his new home as well as the lady currently living in that house to her new flat. This involves extra manpower, so Rob and Mark who are self-employed and work for different removal companies are with us today. I have also hired an additional truck from a company in Park Royal which involves collecting the vehicle at 7am and returning it to them on completion of the removal, so a long day lies ahead.

All is going well on loading the estate agent's house until we are halfway through and he tells me there is a key to the house he must have which was in the hall cupboard drawer. Frustratingly, this was the first thing put on the truck, so it means removing everything off that has been loaded so far to get to the cupboard. What is it with estate agents and keys!

Friday, 20th December 1991

It was a late one last night with some mates meeting up for a Christmas drink, we have two jobs today so have to hire a truck and Mark is coming with me to do a removal in Hampstead. On collecting the hire truck, I am told they are very busy leading up to Christmas and only have a curtain sider available; these are the vehicles with soft sides that can be pulled back to open.

This is not ideal for moving furniture but we have no choice, and what looked like a hard day has just gotten worse. It was a good job that the flat in Hampstead was only moving two roads away as there was a definite shape of furniture pushing through the soft sided truck as we drove along.

Monday, 30th December 1991

Delivering house contents from our store in Pinner to a new flat in Canary Wharf, Central London. There is just myself and Rob as it is not a large removal, although in the days before Sat Nav, it is good to have someone who can read a map with me.

Canary Wharf is still being developed, so we drive to Tower Bridge and eventually find the flats we are looking for. The flat is on the third floor and has a magnificent view over the Thames, even so you could still buy a flat here for £100k as we are in the middle of a recession. Once we have delivered all the furniture, I realise there are six dining chairs in a circle around an empty space, we have managed to leave the dining table behind in the warehouse!

This means another trip back here tomorrow, but as the table is dismantled, I can fit it in the back of my car and deliver it on my own, at least I now know the way.

Friday, 3rd January 1992

Moving from a house in Pinner to a town house in Eastcote, these particular houses have very narrow staircases and being a town house, the settees need to go to the living room on the first floor with the bedrooms being on the second floor. Not surprisingly, the settee will not fit up the stairs, so it has to be lifted over the lounge balcony and in through the French doors. Most people eventually get frustrated with all the stairs once they have lived in a town house for a few years—especially when they have children.

Sunday, 16th February 1992

We don't usually work Sundays but this is the landlord of a pub in Chorleywood that dad has moved several times before, so are willing to make an exception. As with all pubs, the accommodation is an after-thought, so any large furniture is always a problem. The settee has to be taken out of a first-floor window and then carried over a flat roof, before being carried down a fire escape. The couple are moving back in to their own house so delivery is a lot easier at their home in Northwood.

Friday, 20th March 1992

I have been studying for three months to take a Certificate of Professional Competence exam today in order to become a qualified Transport Manager. This is a legal requirement to operate removal vehicles and I pass the test.

Monday, 30th March to Wednesday, 1st April 1992

This is a large house in Pinner moving to Wotton-under-Edge in Gloucestershire.

We spend the first day packing and loading our Bedford truck. The second day we load another large removal truck belonging to a local firm owned by Nigel, and we deliver both trucks the third day.

There are six men unloading both vehicles in to a beautiful cottage with an underground wine cellar. The previous owner left our customer some of his bottles of wine as a moving in present; I have never been in a proper cellar before and am surprised at the different temperature to the rest of the house. At the end of the job the customer asks us to stand in a line like something out of *Downton Abbey*, and presents us with a thank you gift. It is nice to be appreciated for a very difficult job.

Tuesday, 21st April to Wednesday, 22nd April 1992

We are packing and moving a house in Pinner which has subsidence—which is a common problem in this area as the clay soil dries out and causes cracks. This involves packing and moving the entire house including carpets and curtains in to storage for approximately six months, and then returning everything once the work is completed. As it is paid for by the clients' insurance company, there is always a delay in payment, but it can be profitable although very traumatic for the customer. In the garden is a wishing well and I can't resist dropping a coin in to make a wish; we will see what happens in the future.

Monday, 11th May 1992

A previous customer has asked us to move them back to Harrow-on-the-Hill having moved them to Wilmslow, Manchester, a few years ago. We drive up and load on the Monday, returning quite late that evening. The following day we deliver to a flat which was converted from a monastery not far from Harrow school. As with most jobs on "the hill", the access is extremely challenging but we managed to deliver everything without too many dramas.

Saturday, 30th May 1992

We loaded the landlord's possessions from a JJ Moons pub in Harrow yesterday and are driving to Bodmin in Cornwall to deliver today. My dad and I are sharing the driving as it is over 200 miles each way, and Martin is also with us to help with delivery. It is a beautiful sunny day and dad is pointing out all the landmarks along the way, from Stonehenge to the best place for a cream tea in Devon. On arrival, we have the usual problems delivering to another pub and have to take most of the furniture over the roof and in the window.

We finally get back to Ruislip for 9 pm where I am meeting friends and dad drops me off on the way home. We are meeting in another JJ Moons pub before going to a local party; after a quick change of clothes and a few beers, we arrive at the house to find that only one of the four of us had actually been invited, but we gate-crash the party anyway. I was very glad I did as I met my future wife Sheila that night; the wishing well proving to be a powerful force.

Monday, 15th June to Tuesday, 16th June 1992

We load a house in North Harrow and drive to Hayle, Cornwall, where dad and I have booked a bed and breakfast to stay overnight. As this journey is 240 miles each way, it is too far to drive there and back in one day so we have to stay over; it is good to see the town we are moving to for a change as we are normally in and out as quickly as possible and could be anywhere in the country. Our dinner consists of a proper Cornish pasty with a full English breakfast the next day before unloading and driving back to Harrow.

Monday, 29th June 1992

The owner of a local insurance company has asked us to move his grand piano from one house to another—something my dad has been doing for years. He shows me how to remove the legs of the piano and then safely transport using piano wheels. Years later, a specialist piano removal company told me over a cup of tea how they had to move a grand piano from a well-known client's penthouse flat above Harrods in London. This involved closing the road over Easter and bringing the piano down by crane having taken the plate glass window out first.

As they were manoeuvring the piano out of the window of the tenth floor, the men were strapped to the building with safety harnesses for safety; after successfully completing the move, one of the men was boasting how strong he was and pretending to break the harness when it ripped apart in his hands and his face went white as he suddenly realised this was the only thing preventing him from falling ten floors minutes earlier.

Thursday, 30th August to Friday, 31st August 1992

I don't usually move offices, but was able to get a good price for moving this one within Hounslow. We have seven men for the move, together with two trucks, and as many trollies as possible; unlike houses, a lot of office furniture can be pushed on trollies most of the way.

Specialist office removal companies don't like doing house moves for this reason, the downside being most of the work is in the evenings and on weekends; we prefer the interaction with our customers even if it does require more lifting.

Wednesday, 16th September 1992

Black Wednesday: as the stock market crashes, interest rates are raised to 15% and the UK is pushed out of the Exchange Rate Mechanism; Colin rents a room at our office in Pinner Road and we are both about to post the keys to our flats we have let through the Estate Agents doors when interest rates return to a more manageable amount overnight. Ironically this was the beginning of the end of the recession, although business is still tough for the foreseeable future.

Wednesday, 23rd September 1992

We have been asked to work for the BBC who are filming an episode of *Jeeves and Wooster* in a large house in Northwood. Arriving at the house, there is a hive of activity with film crews and all their equipment; our job is to remove surplus furniture from the house to put in to storage and then return the following Saturday once filming is finished. All this for a one-minute scene in a future episode.

Saturday, 17th October 1992

Weekend away to Paris with Sheila: I think she thought it would be warmer than it was as she didn't bring a coat and I spent the weekend freezing after lending her mine.

Friday, 20th November 1992

Removal from Hatch End to Wokingham, Berkshire; we had to wait for the keys to the property, so we were driving along the M4 in the dark on the way home. There was an orange glow in the sky as we approached Windsor; as we got nearer you could see that Windsor Castle was on fire. The turrets of the castle looked like giant chimneys with flames roaring out of the top of them; an unbelievable sight which caused enormous damage. I visited the castle many years later and you would never know that there had been a fire.

Wednesday, 10th February 1993

We arrive at a husband and wife's house for 8.30am to start loading a local move. After working a little while we are offered a cup of tea, so we take a break; at this point the couple join us at the back of the truck where we are sitting; since my dad will always have a smoke with his tea. Suddenly, the lady stops talking, her eyes spin and she falls to the ground like a tree that has just been felled. There is a sickening crack when her head hits the floor and her husband lets out a despairing cry. We immediately get a neighbour to phone for an ambulance and use our furniture blankets to make her comfortable.

Tragically, she has had an aneurysm in the brain that has burst, possibly aggravated by the stress of moving, and died instantly. The removal still has to go ahead as contracts have been exchanged; obviously her husband is not going to be moving in to their new house so the furniture and personal belongings are put in to storage. Later that week, I have the unenviable task of meeting the husband at our warehouse so he can collect his black suit and tie for the funeral. A few weeks later, we have a very solemn removal to perform— moving from storage to the new house where the husband is now living on his own.

Saturday, 27th February 1993

Today we are moving a friend of mine I play squash with from his flat in Ealing to a new house he is buying with his girlfriend in High Wycombe. Chris works out regularly as well as playing squash but soon finds out helping to carry boxes and furniture is a different type of fitness and struggles to keep up, much to our amusement.

Tuesday, 2nd March 1993

Leave Harrow at 7am having loaded the truck yesterday for a removal to Totnes in Devon, we drive along the M4 and take a break before Bristol in a motorway service station. I am aware that the truck is not running well, and on inspection, notice a fuel leak. There is a garage attached to the service station, so I ask a mechanic to take a look; he very kindly takes the time to fix the problem and gets us on our way. I make a note to speak to our regular mechanic who has only just serviced the vehicle.

Thursday, 11th March 1993

We are helping another local removal company today with their move; owned by brothers called Andrews. These pair of characters are five feet tall and used to work in a circus; they are however very good at their jobs and my dad has known them for years, so very happy to help out.

Saturday, 24th April 1993

The news today is that the NatWest Tower in Central London was blown up last night by the IRA. I speak to Rob on Monday about some work for us—to hear he is in the process of emptying the offices on the 66th floor of the NatWest Tower; where there are no windows and no lifts working so everything must be moved down the stairs. Good luck to them moving that into storage.

Friday, 16th July 1993

Our job today is to deliver to a house in Ludlow, Shropshire, the contents of a house we loaded in Ealing yesterday. As today is the completion day, we arrive at the house for lunchtime but there is a delay with the money and therefore the keys will not be released. Our customer is as frustrated as we are and suggests breaking in through an open downstairs bathroom window; as Trevor is the smallest, he is volunteered to try. After climbing a step ladder, he enters head-first through the window with my dad and I holding a leg each and trying not to laugh at the bizarre situation. He manages to enter and unlock the front door and we have just unloaded the last piece of furniture, when a slightly confused estate agent finally arrives with the keys.

Monday, 19th July 1993

Today we have Martin helping with a removal from Northwood to Pinner—part of the job involves dismantling and re-assembling a wardrobe. This is proving harder than we thought when Martin suggests he climb inside the wardrobe and assembles it from the inside, an idea met with much laughter and derision.

Tuesday, 10th August 1993

Moving house contents from Northwood to Northwood; upon delivery of the dining table to the new larger house, the customer complained that a pre-existing scratch on the table was caused by the move. After becoming rude and abusive and insisting the scratch was our fault, my dad took a coin from his pocket and proceeded to scrape it from one end of the table to the other with the words, 'Now that's what I call a scratch.'

Friday, 17th September 1993

Delivering to a top floor flat in Pinner, we are unable to move the large settee up the narrow stairs of the flat. With the help of ladders and web ties, we are able to stand on the flat roof and pull the settee up to the window of the flat and deliver that way. I am not sure health and safety would approve but the customer is very grateful.

Tuesday, 2nd November 1993

This time we are delivering to a house in Chalfont-St-Giles when a piece of furniture will not fit up the stairs; this is an older property with sash windows which can be removed. My dad has done this many times before and shows me how; we then are able to deliver the item of furniture before replacing the window back in the frame. Once the removal is completed, we are back in the truck and about to drive away when I look at the upstairs window, noticing it has been put back the wrong way round—meaning the paint is a different colour on the outside to the other windows. Another lesson in removals hard learnt.

Wednesday, 2nd March 1994

Colin is still renting a room in the house we use as our office; this is the same house my dad grew up in and his parents rented from 1930. We have recently started parking our removal truck in the driveway since having the name of Willis of Harrow Removals & Storage sign written on the side. This is in the days when signwriting is still by hand with paintbrushes and not using transfer stickers; unfortunately, it rained for two weeks when the sign writer had only painted the first five letters of our name on the truck and he only returned to finish the job when it had stopped raining. This resulted in very childlike comments from our competitors; you would have thought he could have added the S of Willis before disappearing.

Our removal job today is Colin's girlfriend, Sue, who lives in Northampton and is moving locally, so we drive there proudly showing off our newly completed sign-written truck.

Saturday, 12th March 1994

The husband-to-be of another friend of Sheila's is moving out of his cottage and needs to store his belongings. We collect them from Chorleywood and deliver in to storage at our warehouse in Pinner.

Even though he is a city trader, that doesn't always translate in to common sense, and he leaves his passport with the house contents being moved in to store. As a guest at our wedding next month, he chooses that moment to ask for it to be found and returned from storage—the answer being a polite no.

Monday, 4th April 1994

Sheila and I get married and go for a week's honeymoon in Sicily; guests from Ireland, Australia and Canada make it a truly international event and a day to remember.

Tuesday, 19th April 1994

The warehouse in Pinner is owned by an elderly Scotsman who has a reputation for being careful with his money. He once charged a builder who had lent his cement mixer to him, a fee for storing the mixer, as he had not collected it quickly enough once no longer required.

The local court was littered with people he had sued for money; I therefore ensure his rent is delivered on time today.

Sunday, 24th July 1994

After spending a few days holidaying in Dublin where my wife is from, we return to City Airport in London to be collected by my parents. Virgin Airways have only just started flying this route and were very accommodating with regards to excess luggage.

We appeared at arrivals with a baggage trolley piled high with wedding presents; consisting of a coffee table, full length candlestick holders and numerous assorted boxes and bags.

Thursday, 4th August 1994

After collecting a regular customer's furniture from Cheshire yesterday, we are delivering to a large cottage in Oxhey today. As this cottage is down a very narrow lane, we have had to hire a small van and shuttle the contents from the large truck parked in the main road down the tight lane. This is a very time-consuming process as everything has to be unloaded, loaded and then unloaded again for delivery.

Monday, 26th September 1994

A friend of mine moved to Southampton a few years ago after living in Ruislip most of his life; he loved his new house, living opposite the cricket ground where he could watch Hampshire play from his bedroom window. His wife, alas, never settled and he has had to give in to the inevitable and move back to Ruislip today.

As property prices in London have risen more than in Southampton, this means moving to a much smaller property in need of a lot of work. Hopefully, they will both be able to settle now, although his wife looks a lot more pleased with their new home than he does.

Friday, 21st October 1994

A local move today within Harrow: the furniture to be moved is a reasonable amount, but the customer also wants to move their carpets and storage heaters.

We have agreed to this although it involves a lot of work at the end of loading to take up the carpets in every room and is a very dirty job. I cannot understand taking the stairs carpet as this will never fit the stairs of the new house; also, the underlay is falling apart as it has not been touched for a long time. The storage heaters are full of bricks that retain the warmth when heated and are very heavy to move—thank heavens for central heating. I have moved customers in to homes where people have taken everything from the doorbell to lightbulbs and even the bath!

Wednesday, 16th November 1994

I arrive at the truck this morning to find someone has stolen the windscreen overnight by cutting the rubber seal holding it in place. We are due at a house in Ruislip for 8.30am, so I decide to drive the few miles necessary without a windscreen and get a new one fitted whilst we are loading at the customer's home.

Apart from being very cold, we are also getting a few strange looks; on the way to the job there is another local removal company driving towards us from the opposite direction ready to start their day. I cannot resist leaning forward out of the front of the truck window to wave—enjoying the confused look on their faces.

Thursday, 15th December 1994

This is a large removal over two days with two trucks to Amersham and this is the second day. Although we have additional men to help, it is a very late finish, and on the way home one of the trucks breaks down driving up a steep hill with a fuel problem that was supposed to have been previously fixed. I think it is time to change the mechanic we use to a new one that a colleague has recommended.

1995 to 1999

Saturday, 28th January 1995

I am delivering a load from our store in Pinner to a very smart address in Chelsea for a barrister previously living in Pinner. The property prices by today's standard are a bargain as we are still in a recession, and it is an interesting part of London by the river that we don't move to very often as not many people can afford to.

Wednesday, 22nd February 1995

I have arranged several appointments with local estate agents to discuss recommending our removal services to their clients. Some are more accommodating than others and want to know what benefit it is to them; although our company is well established with an excellent reputation and could help their clients, the bottom line is usually about money.

Friday, 17th March 1995

Today I am joining the modern world by buying my first mobile phone for work; although not as large as some I have seen being used in the local café which were the size of a car battery, this is still not much smaller than a brick. On a good day the battery lasts six hours, but at least I have some contact with the outside world whilst working out of the office.

Monday, 10th April 1995

Whilst waiting for the solicitors to release the keys of a house in West Hampstead, we are parked on a main road when a car speeds past just as a driver opens his car door to get out. The speeding car takes the other drivers' door clean off, narrowly missing him, and continues without stopping before anyone realises what has happened. I have seen a lot of near misses with drivers and passengers carelessly opening car doors, but this is the first time I have seen one hit.

Friday, 26th May 1995

Sheila and I are buying our first house together and the removal today is in to our new home; we only have a few items so the truck is much too big, but we are both very excited. I have had to rent out the flat we were living in as the continuing recession makes selling it impossible, so I have also become a reluctant landlord.

As our new house had previously been rented, there is a lot of cleaning and maintenance to do before our housewarming party on Sunday—which is also my birthday. Sheila has organised a cake in the shape of our new house, and the good weather means we can enjoy entertaining in our own garden.

Friday, 16th June 1995

I have to attend a meeting with the Traffic Commissioner in Eastbourne today as the final part in getting an Operator's

Licence to manage a removal company. It is a bit like a courtroom, although at least today I am not on trial, only to produce relevant documents for my application.

Although the commissioner is very stern, I am not in trouble, and have done enough to get my new licence in the near future.

Thursday, 25th July 1995

We are working for Harrow School today, moving one of their masters from one school house to a larger house within Harrow-on-the-Hill. This is a regular occurrence every summer holiday for school masters to move between properties owned by Harrow School.

I don't usually get these jobs as they are always looking for the cheapest quote; even though school fees here are in excess of £40,000 per year each pupil. When I ask the bursar for payment at the end of the removal, he informs me that this is not how they do business and will make the payment in due course (three months later).

Monday, 7th August 1995

An unusual removal today within an art deco development of flats in pinner; when these flats were originally built, they not only had an outdoor tennis court but also a dance floor for residents' use. Today I am moving an elderly lady living on the second floor (these flats have no lifts); she is swapping flats with a younger lady living on the ground floor who we are also moving.

The attraction of the ground floor flat is obvious for the older lady, and the second floor flat has a beautiful roof garden; so they are both very pleased with the swap. A truck is not necessary and four men move furniture in both directions at the same time like a trail of ants which involves a lot of walking. Today a fit bit will record 20,000 steps for the average removal.

Wednesday, 13th September 1995

I have been exploring the overseas removals market and today we are moving a house from Hampstead to Brittany in France, in partnership with an International Removal Company. The collection goes according to plan, and we can track the vehicle journey on its way to France—something completely amazing to me as this is before Sat Nav became commonplace.

Thursday, 26th October 1995

This time we are helping to load a house in Harrow that is moving to Northern Ireland; again, in co-operation with an Irish removal company, we are able to perform the removal as economically as possible for our client without having to use our own vehicle. The company I am using have a large warehouse in Belfast where they will transfer the furniture to, before delivering to the customer's new house.

Apparently, they tell me that calming music is played in the warehouse to create a good atmosphere; possibly so the furniture doesn't get too stressed.

Monday, 27th November 1995

Our journey today is to Sheringham on the Norfolk coast, a very picturesque area although very windy at this time of year. There is still a good transport café halfway there, so we stop for a full English breakfast before continuing through the beautiful countryside. The wind is getting quite strong and being a high sided vehicle means the truck is blown about on the road; my Uncle's truck was blown off the road in to a ditch a few years ago so I am very aware of strong winds.

I notice a water leak as we are leaving the café from the front of the engine, so I look for the nearest industrial estate we can stop where there might be a mechanic who can help. I manage to find someone but to get to the leak for repair involves tipping the cab of the truck; this would be alright if the Luton part over the cab of the truck didn't need to be empty. We therefore have to empty the majority of the furniture from the back before a repair can be made, and then reload to get on our way.

Tuesday, 19ᵗʰ December 1995

I have hired a smaller truck today which my dad and Trevor are going to drive to Yorkshire and back in the one day; this is a return journey of 400 miles, so it will be a long day for them both. Dad used to have to stay overnight for much smaller distances, but with faster vehicles and better motorways the journey times are much better.

Saturday, 13ᵗʰ January 1996

I have had printed some change of address cards, with our company name on, for distribution to people who are looking to move or for our customers who have just moved in to their new home. In the days when text messages and emails were not commonplace, people still informed their friends and family by post of their new address. It is also normal on moving day for the gas and electric companies to send someone to your home to take a final meter reading, instead of having to do this yourself, either over the phone or online.

Thursday, 14th March 1996

We are moving a family in to a house which requires some modernisation; on arrival at the new property, we discover that the old man living there on his own did not realise that he had to move out on the day of completion. Our truck is full of our client's furniture and belongings as well as their new house also being full of the previous owners' furniture and belongings. As the money has been transferred in to his solicitor's account, he no longer owns the house but is still sitting in his favourite chair refusing to move.

After some delicate negotiations, the compromise is for us to move his furniture to one side of each room and store our customers' furniture on the other side, whilst he arranges for someone to move him out the next day.

It is amazing that no one takes the time to explain to him how the moving process works, or to support an older person in what can be a very stressful and difficult process. Our customer is very understanding; although I don't think they were expecting to inherit a lodger on the first night in their new home.

Thursday, 9th May 1996

After loading the entire contents of a three-bedroom house in Harrow for removal to Surrey, the customer receives a phone call from their solicitor to say there is a problem with the money being transferred by their buyer. I decide to wait at the property before driving to Surrey until the problem is resolved. The money never arrives, so after having said their goodbyes to all the neighbours, we have to unload the contents of the truck back in to the same house we moved them out of that morning.

A heart-breaking situation for the couple intending to move, and something that happens at least once a year due to the dysfunctional system of buying and selling properties.

Friday, 19th July 1996

Today we are moving a retired couple about twenty miles out of London in to a 19th century cottage set in a picturesque village; the husband is over six feet tall, and has already been to the cottage which they already own. Whilst exploring their new home yesterday, he realised that the five-foot door frames may cause a problem when he knocked himself out walking in to one. The plan is now to lower the floors where possible or put padding over the door frame.

Thursday, 1st August 1996

This is an interesting day as we have two moves in and out of store, and an Irish friend of Sheila's is moving back home. I have arranged for an Irish company to collect and deliver their furniture, so when I get a phone call from the lady moving, I guess all is not well.

'They won't take the children's play house,' she says, sounding quite annoyed. It appears they were unable to dismantle it, so my dad and Trevor go to lend a hand and dismantle it in no time.

The truck then catches the ferry the following day, and delivers to Ireland the next week—children's play house included.

Thursday, 15ᵗʰ August 1996

Another friend from Ealing is moving his family to Kent; he is a music teacher so he has a lot of books, and I used to work with his wife so it is sad to see them go.

They have a young family which is the main reason for moving out of London to a more rural setting. Brian famously played the funeral march on the organ at my wedding.

'Don't expect me to move all those bloody books upstairs,' I say by way of retribution.

Friday, 30ᵗʰ August 1996

'That guy used to be the drummer for *The Sweet,*' Trevor says, as a man wearing a bomber jacket with the words "Gorky Park" emblazoned on the back walks out of the house next door to the one we are moving. This was a band in the 1970s, and very much Trevor's era as he is the only person I know to get married in a crushed velvet brown suit with huge collars and even bigger flares. Very much of its time.

Thursday, 17ᵗʰ October 1996

A client of ours has bought the contents of a bankrupt hotel which they want moved to different parts of the country. Whilst we have the relatively straightforward job of delivering beds to Norfolk, I have arranged for a larger national removal company to move the industrial kitchen to Preston. I think we got the better of the deal, although the damage caused moving the kitchen results in a considerable insurance claim at a later date.

Monday, 11th November 1996

Our regular clients sometimes ask for larger items of furniture to be delivered to an auction house; one such lady has asked for an antique grandfather clock to be delivered to Christie's auction house in Central London. The removal of these clocks requires the weights, pendulum and clock face to be removed and is a delicate task. On arrival at the auction house, there is a fascinating collection of items to be sold, some magnificent antique chests of drawers are being sold for very little money as they are not fashionable any more.

Tuesday, 10th December 1996

Our crew consists of Tony who is very good at dismantling and assembling flat pack furniture. This is particularly useful today as the customer wants to bring two fitted wardrobes with them which require complete dismantling. Whilst delivering to a house in a none too salubrious part of London, Tony's jacket is stolen from our truck with his house keys inside. He recovers the jacket discarded nearby but the keys are gone; I will have to ensure the cab is locked in the future as I have always thought us to be safe whilst working nearby.

Thursday, 2nd January 1997

Not a very good start to the new year as we are moving two men in to storage whilst their insurance company make good damage caused by roots to their house from a tree nearby. The CCTV cameras outside the front door of their home should have been a clue that this couple were going to be difficult.

As the insurance company were paying, they were determined to get as much as possible out of the move and not in a nice way. I later found out from a neighbour that she had seen the men hitting the cracks in the wall of their house with a hammer in order to make the cracks as bad as possible and force the insurance company to pay out. As Tony warned me earlier, 'Don't trust these pricks,' it seems he is a good judge of character.

Wednesday, 14th January 1997

A very cold and icy day and I am moving a lady that dad has moved several times before; he is not here though as currently on holiday with my mum in the warmth of Australia visiting my brother. Not that I am jealous at all, but did I mention it is freezing here?

Although the move is only a short distance, it is going to the 7th floor of a block of flats, there are two lifts but only one is working. It is dark by the time we have finished, and even the furniture feels freezing cold as it is taken in to the flat, not to mention our hands and feet.

Tuesday, 21st January 1997

Another giant leap in to the modern world is taken today with the delivery of my first computer; Sheila works for IBM so that was the obvious choice, although the size of the monitor is huge compared to the small screen size.

I will now be able to dispense with the typewriter we have always used at my nan's old kitchen table, and sit at my desk trying to learn how it all works. We still have the original Texas Instruments calculator that dad bought which he thought at the time was a marvellous invention.

Friday, 14th February 1997

I have taken a day's holiday so Sheila and I can spend valentine's day together instead of working as we normally do. We have booked a trip to the Kent coast and back on the Orient Express, lunch included. A lot of people have dressed like something out of an *Agatha Christie* film for the occasion, it certainly makes a pleasant change from moving furniture on a Friday.

Monday, 19th May 1997

A friend of mine has contacted me to say his mate needs help moving his girlfriend out of her house and in to his. As her house is hard to find in Buckinghamshire, I arrange to meet him en route so he can guide me to it; what he doesn't say is that his mate's girlfriend is married and her husband does not know she is moving today.

He is also unaware that she is taking most of the furniture with her, and is going to get quite a shock on returning home from his city job tonight. Everything is packed and loaded at a faster pace than usual, and we make our escape without any awkward questions from the neighbours.

Friday, 6th June 1997

Another friend is selling his house after getting divorced, this time with his wife's knowledge, and needs a few items collected and delivered to his new flat. Trevor and I drive to Oxfordshire where his ex-wife is waiting and looks less than pleased that we are taking anything; at one point coming in to the back of the truck to reclaim a frying pan she insists is hers. There is not a lot to load so it does not take long; however, on trying to start the Bedford truck, it is apparent the battery is flat. We are parked in a very small village on a slight downslope, 'I've got an idea, Trev,' I say, 'let's push start it!'

As he is putting his back in to it, an old lady walks past and asks if she can help. Between them, they get the wheels rolling enough to jump start the truck and we carry on with the lady waving us on our way.

On arrival back in London we unload in to the flat without turning the engine off, and then make it back home to have a new battery fitted the next day.

Tuesday, 10th June 1997

We sometimes work for a local hotel—moving furniture from room to room or in to storage as required. Today seems a particularly pointless task as we are asked to swap identical furniture from one room to another, looking exactly the same at the end as it did when we started. I am sure there is a good reason but I can't see what it is.

Wednesday, 17th December 1997

This move from a flat in Ealing is difficult to access as it is a converted house made in to four flats; the first job is to remove the front door or no furniture will come out. Even then, a wardrobe has to be lowered from the first-floor window using ladders and webbing we have brought for that purpose. The front door then proves difficult to put back on properly, proving that sometimes the smallest of removals can often be the most challenging.

Friday, 20th February 1998

'We have an easy job today,' I say to dad and Trevor, 'collecting a few items of furniture from the flat of an old lady who has died and delivering them to her son's house.'

On arrival at her flat we are met by the son who asks for a favour. 'Can you deliver the double bed mattress to an address in Northwood?' he asks.

As this is on the way to his house, I say that this is not a problem, and make sure we load the mattress last so it can be delivered first. The address he gives me is an estate agent in Northwood, so I assume he either owns the agency or is delivering to a friend.

We park outside the estate agent where Trevor and I unload the mattress and carry it through their front door. I should have guessed something was wrong when our customer was watching from across the road just laughing. 'What are you doing with that!' said one of the estate agents.

'I've been asked to deliver it to you,' I said, walking out of the door as quickly as possible since something was obviously wrong. On arrival at our customer's house, he apologised and I asked what was going on. He explained that the estate agency had been renting his mum's flat for him whilst he was trying to sell it. They hadn't been very particular as to whom they rented it to; and as a result, it was being used for prostitution purposes, resulting in multiple complaints to him from his mum's old neighbours.

Delivering the offending mattress to this estate agent was his way of getting even, I'm glad I was able to help.

Monday, 18th May 1998

Moving another friend of mine from Hanwell in West London to storage; since he and his wife have outgrown their flat with the arrival of their first baby. We are storing the contents whilst they wait for their new house to be ready; although I had visited the flat before, I never noticed that they were opposite the rear entrance to a funeral home. As we were loading furniture in to our truck, they were loading coffins in to their hearse; I can now see why they may not wish to raise a family here.

Thursday, 18th June 1998

We have a new mechanic in Hayes who is servicing our truck today, so I am delivering it to his garage early in the morning to leave it with him. As I enter his workshop, there is Paul covered in what can only be described as shit.

'What the hell happened to you Paul!' I say, covering my nose and inching slowly away from him.

He explains that whilst servicing a sewage truck he accidentally undid the wrong hose whilst working underneath the vehicle, only to have the contents of the sewage container spew out all over him. I back away even further while trying desperately not to laugh, and say I will collect my truck later today once he has had a shower.

Monday, 3rd August 1998

Our job today is to fully load a house in Rayners Lane that is to be moved to Barnstaple, Devon tomorrow. HMRC have also chosen this day to inspect our VAT books at 10am, so I have to leave the others loading the truck whilst I return to our office in North Harrow to meet the inspector. Once I have given him all the books, he sits down at what was my grandmother's dining table to go through them all. Our office is actually the house my dad grew up in and our family have rented it since 1930; the landlord has made very little effort to repair or decorate so it still looks very much as it did when my grandmother lived here. The office therefore comprises a dining table, fireside chairs and a TV; since the inspector is going to be here a while, I leave him to get on with it and go back to help finish loading our truck. On returning after a couple of hours I see the VAT inspector has finished early and made himself comfortable; he is asleep in the chair with the TV on—not a very professional look. He is obviously embarrassed and I am not about to make him feel any better; on reviewing the books he has only found a few discrepancies to cover the cost of his visit and cannot get out of our house quick enough.

Thursday, 6th August 1998

As well as my grandmother's house serving as our office, we have also parked the Bedford truck in the driveway for the last few years. This is not entirely suitable as the drive is really only meant for cars and not a forty-foot-long removal truck. I have now found a yard in Wealdstone which is used by an assortment of businesses. Dave, who owns a vehicle rental firm has agreed to sub-let a parking space in his section of the yard. He is a bit of a character and upon arriving for the first time, we find Dave propping up a thirty-foot container with bricks whilst walking about underneath. Obviously, health and safety hasn't reached here yet, but the yard is much more suitable and will prove to be our home for over twenty years.

Thursday, 10th September 1998

While I am away on holiday my dad has asked a local man with his own small van to help with a job. Conor used to be a school teacher who has now retired and does small removals when not returning to his native Ireland. He is a nice guy and a reliable worker, but confesses that our jobs are too hard for him at his age, and although being a great help he would prefer to stick to the small moves.

Monday, 28th September 1998

The end of an era: the lease on our property in North Harrow has finished, so we have to move out after being in the family for sixty-eight years. I will be working from home for a while until we can find a suitable place to use as an office. At least we have a new parking space for the truck, which being a locked gated yard is much better than we previously had.

Friday, 30th October 1998

This is quite a large removal so we started packing and emptying the loft space yesterday; the person we are moving is out of the country, so his parents are helping his wife with the move. I realised he was a cricketer when removing countless bags and equipment from the loft space, it is unbelievable how much complimentary gear is given to top class cricket players.

It became obvious who the England cricketer was when packing signs on the wall stating 'Beware the Ramps', and his proud parents were happy to tell stories of their son's achievements.

Tuesday, 26th January 1999

Although this is a normal house removal from Harrow to Amersham, there is only Trevor and myself fit enough to work, and I am not feeling well either. On arrival at the new house there is the usual delay with the keys being released by the solicitor.

We don't get started until it is dark, and the client hasn't told us that the new property is up a steep fifty-yard-long slope which is inaccessible for our truck. It is late by the time we finish and we both feel utterly exhausted, moving at this time of year can be very challenging.

Friday, 19th March 1999

A local move within Pinner today but the client has a large safe and although we regularly move heavy pianos, I get a specialist safe moving company for this. We have moved smaller safes in the past, but recently a local removal company's employee lost a finger when it was trapped underneath a safe, and I value my fingers and toes too much to take a chance.

Wednesday, 26th May 1999

An old school friend of mine has contacted us as his mum is looking to move house; he is now in the antique trade so could prove mutually beneficial. I remember at school he was planning to work as a stockbroker in the city; rarely do any of us end up where we expected to.

Monday, 21st June 1999

I have a small local move to do this morning and then Sheila and I have tickets to Wimbledon Tennis Championships this afternoon. A great day out as we are welcomed at the nearest train station to Wimbledon by an umpire sitting in his chair on a platform decked out in green astro turf. We are there until late evening and it feels like I have been on holiday for a week.

Friday, 2nd July 1999

Moving an elderly lady today from her house in Harrow Weald to a local bungalow; this is the second person we have moved recently after their partner has had an accident.

This lady's husband fell from a ladder whilst trying to fix the guttering of the house and is still in hospital; last month a middle-aged woman tripped over her dressing gown whilst rushing to answer the front door bell. After falling down the stairs she is now in a wheel chair and also had to be moved in to a bungalow for ease of access.

Saturday, 31st July 1999

A meeting today with a man who is going to create a website and email address for our company; another development we need to embrace along with the computer and mobile phone. A long way from when my dad bought his first calculator in the 1970s for £40.

Friday, 10th September 1999

There are new tenants at our yard who are now sub-letting the parking space to us; Darren is the son and Alan is his dad; both seem likeable people. My dad is in the yard, cleaning and polishing the truck, something he has always taken pride in with all his vehicles. Alan comments:

'You shouldn't be out in this weather, Don, old fellas like us go rusty in the rain.'

Alan is another character who used to be a London cabbie, and likes to tell you about all the people he has had in the back of his cab.

Saturday, 18th September 1999

Dad is recovering from a heart bypass operation he had in the summer, so we decide to treat him and mum to a long weekend in Cork. They fly out today and I am sure the Irish hospitality, as well as excellent food and drink, will help with the recovery and make both of them feel refreshed.

Tuesday, 12th October 1999

Our son Kylam comes to live with us today—after Sheila and I take him to my parents' house, Dad says: 'Fourth generation Willis Removals.' We will see what the future brings, but lovely to see them both so proud.

Monday, 6th December 1999

John is working for the first time with us today, he is a big Chelsea fan and very excited that his first job in Pinner is moving from a home called Chelsea House. It is a large property which we have been packing and preparing for two days, there is still a lot of work to do but all goes according to plan and he proves to be a good and reliable worker.

Thursday, 9th December 1999

We are moving an old customer of Dad's to Norfolk today using two trucks, one of which Mark is driving and I am driving the other. There are 16 people in this chain of moves, and not surprisingly they have been trying to move for some time.

At one point the people at the top of the chain all joined together to buy the flat at the bottom of the chain themselves—after the person's buyer had pulled out. On arrival in Norfolk there is the expected delay with the money making its way through the chain of solicitors, until it finally reaches us at 4 pm and we can start unloading. The owner has to hang fairy lights around the pathway so we can see where we are going.

The journey home is no less eventful with the Department of Transport deciding to carry out a stop check at 8 pm and asking us to follow them to a nearby industrial estate to check the maintenance of our vehicle. The mechanic commented that older trucks are often better maintained than the new ones, which proved to be the case with ours and we could finally make it home.

2000 to 2005

Monday, 17th January 2000

The warehouse in Pinner which we have been using for years is going to become a barn conversion, so I have found more suitable storage in Park Royal. This removal company has a large, modern warehouse which they rent out for trade storage using wooden containers to store the furniture in. We are collecting our customers' belongings today when the crew loading their truck next to us let out a scream; someone has dressed up a skeleton and left it as the first thing you see when opening the container.

The warehouse staff working here are very professional and hardworking, but good to see they still have a sense of humour.

Friday, 4th February 2000

Today is moving an office from Bushey to Edgware, first to second floor without a lift either end. It is a cold day and dad is not feeling well so makes for a difficult move; he promises me he will visit the doctor next week as he has been feeling unwell for a while.

Monday, 28th February 2000

Dad has been admitted to hospital, so after finishing work today I have gone to visit; the news is not good as he has been diagnosed with pancreatic cancer which is inoperable. At least they are letting him home soon—I am lucky to have been able to spend as much time with him as I have in the last few years.

Thursday, 30th March to Saturday, 1st April 2000

The solicitor my family use is moving his offices to merge with a larger firm of solicitors, my dad has moved him several times previously. This involves moving office furniture internally at the new premises to make room for the main removal on Saturday. A friend of mine, Nigel, is working with us today; as a resting actor he is sometimes available to help us out. Nigel is over six feet tall, so I naturally give him the job of moving archive boxes within the loft space of the new office to create more room. Although only the end of March, it is like a sauna up there and he emerges after a few hours, dripping with sweat, to tell me he has an audition to go to in Central London.

'What's it for?' I ask.

'A commercial set in the Sahara Desert,' he says.

'Well, at least you have the right look for it!'

The next day we return to our client's office to move his archive boxes, he takes me to an outside store room which is flooded with six inches of water after recent heavy rain. Although the files are all in the dry on metal racking, we have to wade through the water to bring them all out. From desert conditions to floods, this sums up the environment we sometimes have to work in.

Friday, 14th April 2000

Nigel is again helping with a local move; part of our job often involves un plumbing kitchen machines, and John is trying to disconnect the washing machine. The water pipe will not turn off fully, so water starts to gush out of the back of the washer all over the kitchen. I quickly ask our customer where the emergency water stop tap is to prevent any further leakage; after telling me it is in the downstairs toilet, I rush to find it, only to discover that Nigel has occupied the downstairs loo for his morning rituals.

'Get out of the toilet, Nigel, quickly!' everyone is shouting.

After a long minute, he exits looking confused, and I have to crawl around inside looking for the stop tap; not the most glamorous of jobs but at least we were able to halt the leak of water.

Thursday, 29th June 2000

We are hiring a smaller truck for this removal as the access to both the properties is very challenging. The small truck is used to shuttle the furniture and belongings along a narrow drive to the waiting Bedford truck where they are then transferred. This is obviously very time consuming, so it requires extra manpower;

The doctor we are moving and her husband do not help by making requests such as wanting to move the water butt complete with the rainwater.

'But that's good water,' the husband says when told it would be too heavy to move with the water still inside.

On arrival at the new house, it is a very difficult process to manoeuvre our large truck through the five-bar gate and down a steep tree-lined drive to the new property. So much so that the well-known removal company moving the previous owners out were unable to exit the driveway fully loaded and had to reload on to two smaller vehicles. A heavy concrete grass roller leaves the truck, at one point unaccompanied, flying down the steep slope and narrowly missing John before crashing in to the tyre of the rented vehicle. The best laid plans do not always work.

Monday, 4th September 2000

Our customer today is moving his family to Stevenage before the start of the new school year—both children are excited about starting their new school later this week. After everything is loaded on to the truck, he receives a phone call from his solicitor saying the buyer is refusing to complete on the purchase of the property unless he drops the price by £10,000.

This is obviously blackmail, as not only are the kids starting their new schools but the husband has a new job, all of which they are committed to in Stevenage. I would like to say he told them where to go, but he decided to lose the money for the sake of his family and to avoid the disruption not moving would have caused. Another example of the corrupt system when it comes to moving home.

Monday, 16th October 2000

Dad's funeral today, died aged 69. He lived a very full life and will be missed by all who knew him.

Friday, 3rd November 2000

This is an unusual house move from Rayners Lane to Pinner as the older couple own the terrace properties side by side having broken through the connecting wall to make them into one. The customer has been lied to by various potential buyers, with one person offering to buy their house whilst also proceeding with another house purchase in unison through a different estate agent. They then completed on whichever property would drop the purchase price the most at the point of sale, which I am glad to say wasn't our client. They are now moving anyway and will convert the houses back in to two separate properties to sell individually.

Thursday, 25th January 2001

Travelling today to Windsor for a removal from a flat to another local flat. We moved this man here a few years ago which is why he has phoned us and not a local firm. I remember moving him here from Harrow last time, so it is a surprise to see he has lost an arm since the last time we helped with his removal.

He is now going to a more suitable flat for his disability, and has also changed cars to a specially adapted one.

'I passed out one day in the flat,' he explained, 'my arm was trapped behind the radiator for several hours after I fell.'

He is remarkably upbeat about the whole experience, and making positive changes to get his life back on track.

Monday, 26th February 2001

We are delivering to Gloucestershire today after loading Saturday, a picturesque spot by the River Severn in the Forest of Dean. Our customers have bought a bed and breakfast business and are starting an exciting new chapter in their lives. They are understandably nervous, especially as moving in the middle of a foot-and-mouth outbreak which has resulted in all their bookings for the upcoming Cheltenham Festival next month being cancelled.

'We are doing this for the long term,' is their attitude, and I hope it all works out for them. The previous owners give them two hours handover and then they are on their own; looking after the existing guests that are currently staying at the B & B.

Friday, 18th May 2001

Our customers are very excited to be moving from a three-bedroom house in Northwood to a six-bedroom mansion in Northwood with an indoor pool. The husband has explained that the new house belonged to a builder who has gone bankrupt during the recession; this enables him to buy the new house for a bargain price as a repossession from the bank.

On arrival we are given a guided tour of the house—ending up by the indoor pool which is empty except for a pile of concrete in the middle. The builder was so annoyed with the bank for repossessing his home that he dumped a pile of cement in the swimming pool as well as stripping out light fittings, toilets and sinks before leaving. I assume the price our client paid reflects the damage left by the previous owner.

Friday, 20th July 2001

A husband and wife are moving to a smaller property outside of London now that their children have all left home. Arriving for 8am at the house, I am met at the front door by a very distressed man; he tells me his wife was taken ill during the night and he has left her in hospital; returning home to move house.

His daughter arrives during the morning for moral support, and whilst still loading his belongings, he receives a phone call from his son at the hospital informing him that his wife has died. A terrible situation for everyone; he has to then go to the hospital, leaving us to finish the removal before returning later in the day at his new home.

Thursday, 26th July to Friday, 27th July 2001

Our customer is moving to Cornwall and the distance is too far to be able to drive there and back in one day. We therefore load the truck and drive to the new house—having arranged to stay in a Cornish bed and breakfast, the husband of which collects us by car and drives the three of us to our accommodation.

The car is full of hay and smells of manure, but we are not in the city now; and the B & B is very welcoming—run by the young man and his wife.

Mark, a friend of mine, lives in Cornwall, so he drives to collect us and take us back to his house, where his wife cooks a lovely meal; then drives back to the B & B later.

The next morning, we are cooked a magnificent full English breakfast with fresh eggs collected from the hens running about in the garden. We are then driven back through the narrow lanes to our customer's house to unload the truck before beginning the long drive back to London.

On the way home the Bedford engine starts to overheat, and I have to stop in a lay by to cool it off, fill up with water and then eventually make it home.

Monday, 30th July 2001

After loading a house in Harrow for delivery to Manchester tomorrow, I notice water pouring out of the radiator. Managing to drive over to Paul, our mechanic, he diagnoses a broken water pump and says he will fit a new one overnight before our journey tomorrow. Paul prefers to work at night during the hot summer months as he is a big lad, and drinks a crate of fizzy drinks every day to quench his thirst. True to his word, the truck is ready for collection 7am the next morning and we are able to drive to Manchester on Tuesday, as well as to the south coast on Wednesday and to Devon on Thursday.

Tuesday, 11th September 2001

A normal day packing the glass and china for a lady on her own in Harrow Weald becomes extraordinary when my wife phones: 'Turn the TV on, now,' she says, 'a plane has just flown in to the twin towers.'

Sheila and I had been to the Windows of the World at the top of the twin towers, New York a few years earlier for St. Patrick's Day, so I knew where she was talking about. I asked our client to turn the TV on; we both stared in shock as a plane hit the second tower, and watched the terrible aftermath of both towers collapsing unfold.

Wednesday, 26th September 2001

Driving to our warehouse in Park Royal takes us past a roadside café on the large industrial estate. The lady who runs it makes a fantastic sausage or bacon sandwich and we always stop here on the way to the store. She tells me today that she is emigrating to Australia with her husband in the near future and will be selling her thriving business. Both her and the sausage sandwich will be sorely missed.

Friday, 5th October 2001

It has been nearly a year since my dad died. By coincidence today we are collecting a retired nun from a retreat in Butlers Cross, Bucks; which is only 200 yards away from the church where his ashes are buried. After loading her belongings, I take a break and walk to the church; I can then lay the flowers I have brought with me on his gravestone which is also my grandmother's grave.

Monday, 29th October 2001

Although there are several men who work on a temporary basis with us, they are not always available as they obviously work for other people as well. On these rare occasions we have to use temporary agency staff which is happening today. Having previously worked for an employment agency, sending temporary staff to work, I know some can be excellent and others not so reliable. Today we have one of the better workers, although he does arrive an hour late having got lost on the way.

Friday, 30th November 2001

Delivering a lady to the Brecon Beacons in Wales which is a very remote mountainous region, and especially bleak at this time of year. She doesn't know anyone here and has moved from Harrow for a complete lifestyle change. If you are happy surrounded by sheep and glorious scenery, when you can see it through the rain, then this is the place to live.

We are navigating our way here with maps, written directions and some help from the local postman—since this is still before Sat Nav and I don't think there would be a signal anyway.

Wednesday, 6th February 2002

The concept of a fitted kitchen being part of the fixtures and fittings of a home is lost on some people; this couple live in a large house and have fallen out with their buyers deciding to move everything that isn't nailed down, and a few things that are. The husband has removed the fitted cooker, fitted fridge, and is in the process of unscrewing a kitchen cupboard.

'I didn't agree to move the whole kitchen when I quoted your move.'

This is lost on him, but since none of these things will fit in the new house, and are just being taken out of spite, I am not going to be part of moving them.

Thursday, 28th February 2002

This is Trevor's last day at work; he had worked for my dad since being volunteered to help by his own dad when working at the family café in his early 20s. Now approaching

60, it is time to give his aching limbs a break, and find something a little easier.

My dad used to delight playing tricks on Trev, but they had a very good relationship and it is sad to see him go.

Saturday, 9th March 2002

There was another removal company in the same yard as us; Dave has decided to stop working for himself and come and work for me. He has two parking spaces and a dilapidated shed, which I am in the process of painting and having re-wired, so I can make it in to an office/ store.

Although not the smartest of surroundings, it gives me a base to work from, store equipment and the option to buy another truck since there is now parking space for two vehicles.

'What are you up to?' Alan asks from the other side of the yard.

At that point an insulation board from the neighbouring builders' yard comes flying over the fence in the strong wind, narrowly missing me and hitting a nearby car.

'Trying to stay alive,' I shout back.

Wednesday, 13th March 2002

It is late afternoon; I am driving to Park Royal to collect a second-hand removal truck which I have bought from the company whose warehouse we use. This has side doors for storage containers to be loaded and unloaded by a fork lift truck without the need for handling the furniture more than once.

This is not the only difference to the Bedford truck—driving the Mercedes takes some getting used to and a 40-foot-long vehicle weighing 17 tonnes requires a fast learning curve.

There is also the issue of it being taller than our current vehicle, which is a potential problem as there is a low bridge near our yard with a similar height. Approaching the bridge slowly, Dave walks ahead of the truck to ensure there is sufficient clearance, which there is by a few inches.

Tuesday, 19th March 2002

Ironically the first job I am doing with the Mercedes truck is from the other side of the road to our yard, in to storage. It is not unusual to move people short distances—having previously moved a family in Ealing to the house next door to their present one. There may be no need for a truck, but the expertise and physical challenges are still the same.

Friday, 5th April 2002

Using both trucks today, Dave is moving someone within Wealdstone while I am already loaded and driving to Exeter, Devon in the Mercedes. After delivering to a retirement home, Sean is reversing me out of a long and winding driveway, but doesn't notice a white post until I have reversed in to it. No harm done but the first of a series of dramas with the journey home.

'Is it me or is it getting hot in here?' I worryingly ask Sean on the journey back home.

The plastic map book resting on the cab shelf was starting to melt when there was a loud pop from the engine compartment our cab sits on top of. Not wanting to panic, Sean and I kept going, and apart from being unusually hot for April, there were no more problems getting back to London. After dropping Sean off near his home, I drove to our mechanic in Hayes to check the vehicle over.

'Just have a look under the cab, Paul.'

'You're on fire!' he shouts, running in to his workshop to return with a fire extinguisher, which he then emptied over the engine compartment of the truck.

A discarded cigarette butt must have been sucked up in to the engine compartment setting alight the insulation between the cab and the engine. Although there were no flames, the wind from driving was fanning a smouldering fire making our cab very hot and uncomfortable. The popping noise was an air pipe exploding as the embers burnt a hole in the plastic and we were actually very fortunate to make it home. As usual, Paul performs his magic and the truck was ready to work again the next day.

Friday, 19th April 2002

It's important to know when to say no.

'You can reverse up our drive over the wooden plank,' our customer said helpfully.

Of course, I should have known that this was not strong enough for a removal truck full of furniture to reverse over. After the rear wheel had crashed in to the ditch covered by the wooden plank, I was very lucky to drive out using first gear, which is hardly ever used with normal driving.

The slope of the driveway was steep and covered in mud where the builders were still finishing renovating the house.

When a builder says he will be finished on a certain day to move in, I have yet to arrive to anything other than a building site. Even brand-new homes are often still painting the front door, or laying the front drive and internal flooring.

Thursday, 20th June 2002

Customers will often underplay the difficulty of access to their new home even when asked specifically if there are any problems. On arriving in Epsom, the entrance for a 200-yard drive is through a narrow gap between two brick walls. Before our customer arrives, the existing owner appears, takes one look at our long removal truck and says:

'You'll not get that up there, I told your bloke to only use small vans for moving in.'

This is not good news, also a little late in the day to be receiving this information; the walk is long and the weather hot. Upon our customer's arrival I suggest he helps push the trollies as he is the reason we have such a long walk; I'm glad to say he was exhausted by the end of the day.

Thursday, 29th August 2002

Fashions in furniture change like any other, meaning the type of household belongings we move are constantly changing. My dad's generation had very different furniture and less personal belongings (especially kids' toys) than today's generation. One item that changes more than most is the T.V and at this time they were becoming heavier and larger than ever before.

The flat screen is still some way off, but people are still wanting 40-inch screens to watch the football on.

Moving this T.V from a first floor flat requires four men, one on each corner, to carry it down the stairs and in to the truck. It is the size of a small fridge and the weight of a washing machine; some fashions are more trouble than others.

Tuesday, 29th October 2002

As containerised storage involves loading wooden crates by fork lift truck, we are collecting some empty containers from the warehouse before driving to the customers' house for loading. This involves attaching a platform to the side of the truck with a ramp leading up to it and then opening the side doors to load directly in to the wooden container.

There is a skill to loading safely and securely, as well as ensuring there is not too much weight in any one container. Recently the warehouse had an accident where one container was filled with heavy books and then stacked on top of four others. As the fork lift driver was trying to lower this down, the weight of the load overturned his truck causing damage to both him and the containers.

Wednesday, 4th December 2002

Our mechanic Paul has offered to replace the uncomfortable driver's seat in the truck with a luxurious leather one he has obtained from a Ford Cortina. This pimped up version is a big improvement—now I will be as comfortable as the other lads who can stretch out in the sleeper pod when travelling on long journeys.

Wednesday, 8th January 2003

The start of a new year has us loading from a first floor flat for delivery to Kent; part of the job involves carrying a very heavy piano down one flight of stairs as there is no lift. We do not arrive at the house in Kent until 2 pm, and there is still no sign of the keys being released, so we have to wait alongside our client until the solicitor has received their money.

We are still waiting when it begins to get dark at 4 pm, until finally, half an hour later, the estate agent phones our customer to say he will hand-deliver the keys as it is late. Another 15 minutes pass until an obvious looking estate agent exits his car and starts walking towards us, patting his jacket pockets all the way.

'He's forgotten the bloody keys,' I say to John.

Sure enough, he had them when leaving the office, but now can't find them, so he has to return to the estate agents to look for them.

He had dropped them in the car park while getting in to his car; eventually we are able to unload our customer's furniture and start the long crawl home around the M25.

Saturday, 1st March 2003

Waiting to take delivery of a land rover which I am leasing for work as an extra vehicle for packing our customers' homes prior to removal.

'Here comes the circus,' we laugh, as the delivery driver takes a mini motorbike out the boot of the car and drives precariously back up the road.

Friday, 23rd May 2003

The young couple are moving from a five-year-old two-bedroom house near our yard to a brand-new property in Northwood. On arrival at the new house, I am amazed to see a six-bedroom mansion set in its own grounds that has been finished to the highest standards. This is a huge step up the property ladder, apparently her husband works in the city as a trader and received a considerable bonus last Christmas.

Monday, 16th June 2003

'I'm moving to a private estate in Ascot,' the lady tells us as we are discussing her new home over a cup of tea. It becomes apparent that the private estate is actually a mobile home park.

'Oh, you're moving to a caravan then,' John says.

'It's not a caravan,' the lady replies.

I will have to give John some lessons in diplomacy.

Thursday, 3rd July 2003

As we are driving towards Oxfordshire in the Mercedes truck, there is a traffic jam in Ruislip which is not moving; people are looking out of first floor windows and there is a lot of activity in the high street. Suddenly a man in a white transit van is seen fighting with another man who is trying to stop him getting back in the van and driving away.

He manages to break free and drive at high speed down the pavement before re-joining the road and crashing in to the front of our truck. He tries to escape but we are out of our cab and stop him leaving until the police arrive.

He looks drunk but apparently had an ischemic attack, or that is what he told the police and insurance company.

I am more concerned with repairing the body work which is now bent over the front wheel as well as the water leak coming from a cracked pipe. We manage to get to our delivery address and then make it home; however, there is a thousand pounds worth of damage which the insurance company refuse liability for due to a medical get-out clause in their policy. There is also the problem of re-arranging work and organising hire vehicles to ensure our customers are still moved on time.

Monday, 21st July 2003

First week of the school holidays and we are working flat out all week with both trucks and all the manpower available. Some jobs are local and some out of the area, but all are families trying to settle their children in to a new home before starting a different school.

There is excitement in the air, especially the young family whose new house incorporates an outdoor swimming pool; I am sure they will be popular over the holidays.

Monday, 11th August 2003

A record heatwave in London today with temperatures reaching 100 degrees Fahrenheit, even starting early it is getting very hot by mid-morning with a lot of water being drunk. Arriving at the new address for lunchtime, we seek out shade wherever it can be found.

I have loaded a chandelier with candles which have now melted to a 90-degree angle. Someone has found the kids' water pistols so while waiting for the keys we can amuse ourselves and cool off at the same time.

Tuesday, 30th September 2003

Time to say goodbye to our Bedford truck as I have traded it for a smaller Ford Iveco—which I am collecting today. This vehicle is newer and more suitable for parking in the narrow roads where we often work; I will be getting it sign-written shortly, although the days of hand painting are finished, transfer stickers are how our name is put on the vehicle now.

Thursday, 9th October 2003

The first opportunity to move a smaller house using our new vehicle to South London; parking is difficult at both ends which is why this truck is more suitable. The journey to south of the river takes an hour, but this is a busy route and the same trip back is over three hours to cover 20 miles.

Fortunately, we don't move many people from North to South London as most stay on their own side of the river.

Monday, 17th November 2003

This has been a difficult removal from the start with more than one piece of furniture causing problems getting out of the house. We finally get on the road to Hertfordshire by late lunchtime, and have been driving for an hour when the mobile phone rings. 'The money isn't going through today,' our customer says.

I turn the truck around and drive back to our yard, the next day moving the furniture in to storage as the customer is not sure when the keys will be available. By Friday they have given up and decide to move everything out of store and back to their original house.

This system of moving house really needs to be overhauled, but as it doesn't affect Tony Blair and his Islington cronies, I won't be holding my breath.

Friday, 28ᵗʰ November 2003

'You will have to move that truck,' shouts a traffic warden in my direction.

We are parked in Marylebone, Central London; although finding anywhere to stop in this part of town is impossible. The traffic warden in question is doing his best impression of a gestapo officer when a helpful policeman intervenes and explains that we are not causing any problem where we are parked and to leave us in peace.

The removal company moving out of the fourth floor flat have currently got a piano stuck halfway down the stairs since it wouldn't fit in the antiquated lift. We begin moving in using the lift, but have our own problem with a large sofa that will neither fit in the lift or go up the stairs. The rest of the customers' belongings are delivered eventually but the sofa has to come home with us; the next day I deliver it to our warehouse and make arrangements for the removal firm in Park Royal to deliver the sofa using their mobile hoist— which is ideal for situations like this.

They deliver it a week later at considerable cost; it involves putting the sofa on a mobile platform and raising it to the fourth floor, then moving it in the flat via the window. I hope it is a comfortable piece of furniture, and they don't intend to change it any time soon.

Friday, 12ᵗʰ December 2003

We are finally moving the customers from last month who had to return to their old home; to everyone's relief the keys are made available at last and we can complete the move started four weeks ago.

Sunday, 21ˢᵗ December 2003

Colin and Sue, friends of mine, are moving to their new house today and have asked me to help. I supply the truck and drive to Northampton where they are moving to a lovely village outside the main town. Trevor is also coming out of retirement to help.

'I can't lift anything too heavy,' Colin says, 'I'm having a hernia operation next week.'

'You might as well get your money's worth then,' I say, handing him a heavy box off the back of the truck.

Thursday, 4ᵗʰ March 2004

Mr P is moving from a small, messy house in Harrow to a similar house in Pinner. He talks a lot of BS about how successful he is and expects us to be impressed about his move to Pinner, a more affluent area. The day after delivery I receive a phone call.

'My washing machine doesn't work,' he says.

'Well, all we did was lift it,' I reply.

He is insistent that we have broken it, so I hand deliver a claim form the next day for our insurance company, checking the make and model of the machine at the same time.

This model was last made 12 years ago, so when the claim form is returned to the insurance company stating it was only a few years old, I am able to advise them differently.

A genuine accident is always covered by our insurance; unfortunately, not everyone is genuine and I am glad to say in this instance the insurance company did not pay out for his claim.

Monday, 24th May 2004

'Morning, Vicar,' I greet our customer, as he was the parish priest who married my brother many years ago.

His move to Harefield involves packing a vast library of books which is not uncommon for vicars, as well as the regulation piano. I have yet to move anyone from the church who doesn't have an excess of books and at least one piano. There was a time when everyone donated their unwanted pianos to the local church, sometimes as a way of not having to move them to their new home. Our priest is moving out of the church-owned house and in to his own home upon taking retirement, well earnt after many years of service.

Friday, 18th June 2004

On arrival at the customer's new home, everything appears to be progressing nicely with the move; our client informs us that the house is now theirs as the money has been transferred through the solicitors, and the removal van hired by the sellers of the property is driving away loaded.

What no one expected was the previous owner insisting on staying in her house to have a shower and dry her hair, whilst making us all wait outside for an hour until she was ready. I am used to people cleaning their home before leaving, but cleaning themselves is a new one on me.

Friday, 2nd and Saturday, 3rd July 2004

It is surprisingly common to move one person out of a property and another one in to the same house, as with this cottage in Harrow-on-the-Hill; unsurprisingly there are problems moving furniture through the small doors and up narrow stairways.

At least we are well prepared when returning the next day—the electric screwdriver gets plenty of use removing doors and dismantling furniture; nineteenth century cottages were not designed to fit twenty first century furniture.

Saturday, 10th July 2004

My next-door neighbour moved out of her house in to storage earlier this year, and then we moved her to a new home in Kent—which is where I am driving to at the moment along with my family as guests at her wedding.

Although the middle of summer, the rain has not stopped all day and we are delayed in a long traffic jam on the M25 caused by flooding. It is still raining on arrival at the church where the wedding service is nearly over, so we decide to stay outside and pretend that we were there the whole time.

The bride and groom, as well as the bridesmaids, are all travelling to the reception in open-top cars and therefore too busy trying to keep dry to notice our absence in the church.

My dad used to have wedding cars for hire together with the removals business; on one occasion attending the wrong church, so this is not the first time our family have been late for a wedding; fortunately, none of his cars were open-topped.

Friday, 16th July 2004

My family and I are driving to Porthleven in Cornwall for our first summer holiday together; the excitement is high although the summer weather has still not improved. On the journey there I have just overtaken one of many caravans when I see in my rear-view mirror the car and caravan jack-knife while attempting to overtake a truck.

Recently on a similar motorway journey with our own truck, the driver of the car in front passed out and veered across three lanes of traffic in to the central reservation; both accidents are a reminder to me of how careful you need to be when driving long distances, especially on motorways.

Monday, 27th September 2004

From Bell End in Worcestershire to Scratchy Bottom in Dorset, I am constantly amused by English place names; today we are moving to Nomansland which is a pretty village in Wiltshire.

Friday, 8th October 2004

This job sometimes involves other skills apart from moving furniture; today being a counsellor joins the list alongside diplomat and cleaner. The parents of two young children living here were tragically killed in a car crash last week; their Uncle and Aunt are now moving them to live at their home in Buckinghamshire. Obviously, this is a very sad time for everyone involved, all we can do is pack the children's bedrooms with care and move them with the utmost respect.

Wednesday, 17ᵗʰ November 2004

'It's important to be patient and polite when dealing with the general public, sometimes we park in front of a person's driveway or block in their car as there is nowhere else to park. Most people understand that moving the truck when asked is preferable to unloading from the other end of the street; although some protect their parking space like a lioness protecting her cub.

We are parked in a car park belonging to some flats in Watford, delivering the contents of four storage containers out of the side of our vehicle. An angry man confronts me as the truck is obstructing his car,

'Move it,' he says, sounding his horn.

I patiently and politely point out that I am happy to move our truck so he can get out of the car park, and equally happy to put his horn where it needs to be surgically removed if he talks to me like that again.

Friday, 17ᵗʰ December 2004

Nearly Christmas and the two sisters moving from their home in Harrow have cooked home-made mince pies. They have lived here all their lives and collected Whitefriars glass from the factory that used to be in Harrow and Wealdstone. A friend of mine worked there as an apprentice when he first left school, but it closed down soon afterwards.

The glassware is now collectable and expensive, so it has to be packed with care—it is literally irreplaceable and a family heirloom.

Saturday, 19th February 2005

I've started the day badly having agreed to our customer's request to remove some boxes and furniture from his loft space. This is an unpleasant job as the loft is dirty and the ladders are not properly fitted to the loft hatch; I have had personal experience of ladders slipping resulting in a fall from the loft, also the hatch opening as Dave was walking underneath hitting him on the head; and on this occasion Sean's foot going through the ceiling.

Although the loft is supposed to be boarded, there are gaps between the roof joists on which his foot has trodden, cracking the ceiling. He didn't go full on Michael Crawford in *Some mothers do 'Ave 'Em*—hanging through the ceiling with his legs dangling, but the crack will still need to be repaired and the day can only get better.

Wednesday, 23rd March 2005

This is a returning customer of ours who has bought a flat in a new development in Pinner; the most important part of the move for him is his fish tank which is both large and heavy. The water and fish have been taken out for moving, and the weight of the fish tank has left indentations in the fitted carpet. He shows me a trick passed on by his mother, putting ice cubes where the carpet is depressed to raise it back up. Some old wives' tales do work and this seems to do the job.

At least he doesn't ask us to take the fish. I have had previous customers put pond fish in a water barrel and want them moved in the truck.

Friday, 1ˢᵗ April 2005

Looking out over Ascot racecourse on a spring day, there are worse places I could be working, although unloading in to the new house involves a long walk from the truck to the front door. There are five of us working, using sack barrows and trollies where possible, but a lot of the furniture has to be carried by hand as there is no easy way to move it. This is still very much a manual handling job; we will be waiting a long time for automatons to help out.

Thursday, 19ᵗʰ May 2005

The annual MOT for our Mercedes truck is due before it is taken for testing, needing to be jet washed clean underneath as well as serviced by Paul the mechanic. I take it to a place which specialises in this which involves driving over a pit in the ground so they can clean underneath. This is a small yard with a large hole in the ground and involves keeping your nerve and trusting the man guiding you over the pit not to let your wheels fall down the hole.

Afterwards Paul has some minor repairs to make which include extending the rear mud flap by two millimetres as regulations have recently changed before it can pass. Regular checks must also be made every eight weeks to comply with Department of Transport guidelines.

Wednesday, 25th May 2005

'That's God's waiting room,' my dad used to say when moving anyone to Eastbourne on the South Coast. We are taking an older couple there today. On arriving in town, I am struck by how many mobility scooters there are, then notice a mobile repair van specialising in these scooters. Only here could a mechanic offer a mobile service to repair mobility scooters and make a good living; the bonus for us is our customers will usually buy a bungalow making the move easier as with today.

Monday, 6th June 2005

Self-storage has become very popular with some people, even running businesses out of their storage units; we have an arrangement with a local company who recommend our services and are moving one of their clients today. As the cheaper units are on the first floor, this involves putting all the furniture and boxes on to trollies then pushing them along the corridors and up in the lift. This can be some distance and you feel like leaving a trail of string behind you to remember how to get back to the entrance.

At least when the trollies are empty on the return journey, we can race them back, the loser buying the tea at break time.

Monday, 1st August 2005

Having just returned from a week's holiday, the first job back is to move a family out of their home which is being extended and renovated in to a temporary rented house nearby. A lot of people will move out when renovating their home, as it speeds up the building process and means you are not living in dust for six months.

The downside for us is the builders have usually started before we arrive and don't understand why digging a trench across the driveway and lifting hall floorboards might cause a problem.

Tuesday, 2nd August 2005

Our old neighbours from Pinner Road, North Harrow are moving to Wendover today, having lived next to my grandmother for over 30 years. They are a lovely couple and keep us supplied with tea and biscuits on a continuous basis, stopping only to make bacon sandwiches mid-morning. This is then followed by lunch on arrival in Wendover and afternoon tea later, I'm amazed we can still move to unload the truck.

Friday, 12th August 2005

I had moved this elderly couple in to a second floor flat a few years ago, unfortunately the lift stops before their front door and they have six steps still to climb. Since falling ill, this has become impossible for the husband, so we are moving them to the next block on the ground floor.

It is surprising how many people over the age of 65 move to flats without a lift, as an insurance policy against old age, a lift is essential.

Monday, 15th to 17th August 2005

'It looks like Kew Gardens in the back of here,' I remark to Dave as we load the last of the plant pots into the back of the Ford truck. A lot of people now have as much to move from their garden as they do their house. On this occasion, we have a truck completely full with outside plants. There is also a dismantled shed to move, although in my dad's time, people also moved coal sheds after first bagging up the coal.

Our client has dug up some plants that were in the garden to take as well as the potted ones. I was just relieved she decided to leave the pets that were buried in the garden; I'm not sure how the new owners will react to the cross above the pet's grave when they explore their new garden.

Friday, 16th September 2005

The children of this couple are now teenagers so are not interested in the home-made swing using a car tyre that hangs at the bottom of the garden. I ask if I can take it for my six-year-old son, and he is thrilled to have it hanging from our walnut tree next to the basketball ring.

Friday, 30th September 2005

Milton Keynes is a new town one hour drive north of London; it is popular as property prices are much cheaper but is still a commutable distance to London. It was built based on the grid system of roads popular in America, and because of this, there are a lot of roundabouts. As we are crossing our tenth roundabout in just over a mile, I am starting to get dizzy when I see the concrete cow Milton Keynes is also famous for.

Monday, 17th October 2005

This man is clearing out his parent's house who have recently died, and has asked us to move the items he wants to keep to his own house in Pinner. We have to use a brush to sweep the dust off the furniture and the house is a mess, even our customer is using a face mask although he doesn't offer us one. I thought he would want to clean the furniture before putting it in his own house with young children, but apparently not. I will help to clean if someone is considerate to us, but I won't be cleaning up this mess and am looking forward to a shower when I get home.

Wednesday, 30th November 2005

It is not only plants and sheds that are moved from the garden now; there is also a long list of children's toys that customers want taken. There is a trampoline which we are taking whole swing, slide, sandpit and a host of plastic play things. Add that to the bird bath, bird feeder and assorted garden tools resulting in as much outside the house as inside. A garden seat once belonging to Lords cricket ground completes the set; once again a second truck is required for the outside alone.

Saturday, 24th December 2005

When moving someone to Stanmore earlier in the year, I discovered a woodland area where there are deer next to the path. This makes a lovely trip out with our son to feed the deer carrots on Christmas Eve, another year over and another just begun.

2006 to 2010

Thursday, 19th January 2006

This man decided to move out of London a few years ago for a better life in Swindon. He has now inherited the family home so decided to move back. We leave early morning as it is a two-hour drive to reach his house. We then have to load everything, bring him back to London and then unload. It is a long day but at least the weather has been kind. When it snows at this time of the year, our job takes a lot longer and travelling is much harder.

Monday, 13th February 2006

After packing the glass and china for tomorrow's job, we drive by car a few miles to another customer who is literally moving across the road, from number 94 to 95. All we require is: a trolley, some tools for dismantling of furniture and a few hours of good weather. Our customer likes the area so when a larger house became available to buy opposite, they decided to go for it. It certainly makes getting to know the neighbours easier, and for our part, there may be a lot of walking but no truck is necessary.

Friday, 24th February 2006

'Did you know we are standing on a nuclear fallout shelter?' I ask John as we are loading our truck in Stanmore. These houses were built on the site of an RAF base. Many years previously, I had a temporary job of delivering carpet tiles to the fallout shelter that was being built here, carrying them through the underground tunnels.

John is more interested in the Chelsea v Manchester City game coming up, that we are both going to. Hopefully Chelsea have more success than we are currently having, trying to get a cup of tea made by our customer.

Friday, 3rd March 2006

Both of our customers today are related as the parents are swapping their house with the son's bungalow. All the furniture still has to be loaded on two separate trucks, since it would get too confusing trying to deliver the one family belongings without first emptying the other.

The elderly parents now have no stairs to worry about, and the younger family have a larger house so everyone is happy. This is the first time I have had to move reclining leather sofas as they are only just becoming fashionable. The manufacturers have not yet realised that they are not only extremely heavy but will not fit into most houses without being dismantled. This is also the case for the American double fridge, taking the doors off. That is the only way to make it fit, an extremely time consuming and difficult job.

Tuesday, 14th March 2006

This must be the new trend; here we are in Ealing moving number 16 to number 18 on the same road. Everything needs to be packed, even though only going next door we can't move glasses and other fragile items one at a time, so the move takes all day. There is also an upright piano which has to be lifted on its end to get out of the doors. The piano wheels make this difficult task much easier, but there is still an art to moving it safely. The kids play us a song once it is in the new home by way of a celebration.

Friday, 24th March 2006

Our journey is to Yeovil in Somerset, so we had to load everything from the house yesterday including the chest freezer. The customer had not run the food supply down, so was worried about it, defrosting overnight and spoiling all the food. I have managed to leave the freezer at the rear of the truck and run an extension lead to our office where it is plugged in overnight. Note to myself: remember to unplug the chest freezer before driving away in the morning.

Tuesday, 11th April 2006

My HGV drivers' licence is coming up for renewal which happens every five years from the age of 45. This involves: a medical at the doctor's surgery, checking your heart, blood pressure, eyesight and various other functions. I understand this is a necessary safety check, but it is still nerve-racking as there will be no way to operate the business if I fail. Looking at some of the truck drivers in the transport cafes makes me feel a lot better and the medical creates no problem.

Tuesday, 6th June 2006

Returning to our office at lunchtime after packing a customer's house that morning, there is a lot of activity on Alan and Darren's side of the yard.

'What's going on, Alan?' I ask.

'Don't ask,' he says.

Apparently, the men who have just finished laying a strip of tarmac for Darren had originally offered to leave some "spare" tarmac they had in their van. He foolishly accepted without realising they were con men. After 20 minutes laying their tarmac instead of just leaving it, a sum of £10,000 was asked for in return.

Darren has now gone to the bank to withdraw the cash as failure to pay will result in some of his very expensive coach windows being smashed when they are left overnight in the yard.

An expensive lesson learned—still the yard looks nice; only another £200,000 to finish the job.

Monday, 12th June 2006

Our favourite block of flats in Hatch End is the destination for this woman. This must be the tenth time I have been here in recent years. There are only two old lifts to move her to the seventh floor, one is not working and the other seems to have a mind of its own, taking us to random floors.

'You will have to bring it all up the stairs,' the woman says smiling.

'You will have to sleep on the floor,' I reply.

The lift holds together until we are finished; only the settee will not fit in, which indeed has to be carried up seven flights of stairs.

Saturday, 5th August 2006

Driving to Devon during the school summer holidays is not the best idea. Doing it on a Saturday is a recipe for disaster but we have no choice. At least leaving at 6am means we are ahead of the worst of the traffic that migrates to the West Country every weekend over the summer. Our destination is a retirement home, but our customer also wants some items taken to a friend who lives over a pub 20 miles away.

The pub is not easy to find as it is in a small village, down some very narrow country lanes. At one point, the truck is touching hedges both sides and I am praying we don't meet any cars coming from the other direction. Eventually, we park outside the busy pub to unload then start the drive home with all the holidaymakers returning from their summer break.

Tuesday, 8th August 2006

I am not a fan of moving vicars as there are always so many books. We have loaded two trucks with them and are now driving to Sheffield in Yorkshire.

'You'll be rewarded in heaven,' Sean says.

That's the least of my worries trying to navigate Sheffield using the customers' written directions, Sat Nav is still not common so we are reliant on map reading and asking the postman. The local community are out in force to welcome the new vicar, at least there will be plenty of tea and cake to keep us going while carrying his books.

Wednesday, 15th November 2006

There is one thing worse than moving a piano and that is a snooker table; it is only half-size but has a slate back and is extremely heavy. Between four men, we lift it on to the piano wheels and push it out of the house and up the ramp into the truck. The Mercedes truck has a sleeper pod so all four of us are able to travel in one vehicle, enabling the manhandling of the snooker table safely into the new property.

Driving home on the motorway, Vince shouts down from the sleeper pod that he needs a comfort break.

'There's nowhere to stop,' I say, 'use the water bottle.'

His aim would need to be very good in a moving vehicle, so he decides he can wait, sprinting out of the truck on arrival back at our yard.

Thursday, 30th November 2006

An already busy day with five men and two separate jobs has been turned on its head with the news "Sheila's mum has died in Ireland", and we have to get back for the funeral. There is no hanging about when someone dies in Ireland, and the removal means something entirely different to what I am used to. Sheila has already gone; I manage to finish my removal just in time to collect Kylam from a family friend and drive to the airport, leaving the rest of the guys to finish their job tomorrow. We are very lucky to have people we can rely on at this difficult time.

Friday, 16th February 2007

A lot of our clients make the move to the New Forest and Bournemouth area on the south coast. We probably move one person there, every six to eight weeks on average. We are in Ferndown near Bournemouth, waiting for the keys to be released by the solicitors for a change. Our customer, who is waiting with us, is getting more and more frustrated as the clock ticks by; eventually deciding to try and open the front door himself.

He knows the previous owner has posted the spare keys through the letterbox, which are now sitting on the doormat, tantalisingly out of reach. Making a fishing rod with a magnet attached, from the contents of his toolbox, he attempts to "catch" the key while I hold a mirror through the letterbox. Amazingly we are successful, just as his wife receives a phone call from the solicitors saying they can now drive to the estate agents and collect the key.

His wife drives to their office while we start unloading in to the now open bungalow.

Tuesday, 22nd May 2007

Spring has sprung with the mornings and evenings becoming much lighter, which is just as well as I am meeting our mechanic Paul in the yard at 6.30am to fix the fuel filter on the Mercedes truck. The pre-filter keeps blocking so he is fitting a new one before we drive to our job at 8am. This should be straightforward but as he is fitting the glass filter, he drops it and the glass breaks; as there is not time to get another, Paul decides to remove the same filter from his own Mercedes and fit it to ours.

This is too much drama for me so early in the morning before we have even started work, but the rest of the day goes smoothly even finishing in daylight.

Wednesday, 18th July 2007

The fish tank is on the move again as the customer we previously moved is now swapping his flat for his mum's house; although he is part-storing some furniture while renovation work is carried out. His mum is much happier in the modern flat, her son and his fish tank have much more space so everyone wins.

Thursday, 9th August 2007

There have been rumours in the property market all summer that there is a downturn on the way. Today, the news is that the banks are in financial trouble and the stock market is falling. This will have a bad effect on us in the future but for today, the drive to Warwickshire takes us past Anne Hathaway's cottage, the home she shared with Shakespeare. That is the interesting side to moving people around the country. Our customers are moving into a nice cottage themselves, although not on the scale we have just seen.

Friday, 14th September 2007

Lifting a fitted carpet is not something we have to do much anymore, as most people now consider them a part of the fixtures and fittings. This lady has a water leak under the lounge floor, so needs all the large furniture and carpet stored for a week while the leak is fixed and repairs made to the floor. It is important to roll the carpet carefully to avoid unnecessary marks when re-laid. I am happy to do that for her and fortunately, know a good carpet fitter who can put it back later.

Wednesday, 26th September 2007

I have finally bought a Sat Nav to help navigate our way around the country; we are using it for the first time driving to Kettering in Northamptonshire. Dave is in control but pushes the wrong part of the screen on our approach to Kettering resulting in me driving past the exit needed. It is only a minor problem; it still seems like magic that we can navigate without a map, something that would have left my dad speechless.

I soon learn not to put too much faith in the directions given, since it will happily send me down a narrow lane with a low bridge just to save 200 yards on the journey distance. It is a great additional tool to have, however, when used with a bit of common sense.

Wednesday, 3rd October 2007

A friend of Sheila's is moving within Harrow. She is very artistic and her husband loves music, so there is a lot of artwork and C.D.'s to be packed and moved. At least the boxes are a lot lighter than the records we used to move; while lifting one box, a mouse ran out from the space behind resulting in his wife running from the house and refusing to return until it was caught. The children found this highly amusing, greatly adding to the excitement of the day.

My mother-in-law once put a mousetrap down when she heard a scrambling noise coming from the kitchen, discovering just in time that the hamster she was looking after for her grandchildren had escaped in the night.

Monday, 3rd December 2007

I have been buying our boxes and packing materials from the same firm for the last ten years. They collect used boxes from factories and then sell them on to trade companies like ours. Recycling at its best; I used to buy new cartons with our name printed on the side, now the printing is likely to be a beer product or biscuit maker. Our customers like the idea as do I, with boxes being used more than once so I am collecting 200 of them from their warehouse this morning.

Friday, 14th March 2008

After a lot of organisation, we are finally starting this job in St. John's Wood near the famous Abbey Road recording studios. I was recommended to this client by a builder I had previously moved, as there is subsidence work and they have to move out for three months. Property prices here are in the millions, and the house they are renting in Hampstead would be similar.

Together with organising the manpower, vehicles and packing beforehand, there is also the London Borough of Camden to deal with. They are by far the worst borough to arrange parking permits with, taking weeks to approve and charging a lot of money for their poor service. Despite having these permits displayed on our windscreens, I am told by a passing traffic warden that we cannot park for more than an hour when unloading. Only some furniture is staying with the customer, the remainder along with all the kitchen units that have been removed is going to storage.

The insurance company are paying a lot of money for this; I have made sure we are also well paid as there is a lot of work involved and the customer is not easy.

Monday, 2nd June 2008

Just as the recession is starting to bite from the financial banking crisis, the low emission zone is introduced in London, meaning both our trucks require a fuel system to be fitted improving their emission standards. This has to be a government-approved company who are charging an extortionate amount of money to make the trucks compliant.

The two fitters have travelled from Manchester and are staying in a hotel while they work on our trucks, probably five star and dining out on the best steaks! Once they have finished my mechanic tidies up their work, and at least we have the paperwork now to continue earning to pay for it.

Monday, 30th June 2008

Dealing with Camden Council once was enough, so now we are returning our customer to his refurbished home in St. John's Wood. I have not bothered to purchase parking permits. After speaking to other Removal Companies, who regularly work in this borough, I am doing what they do; get a parking ticket and pay the fine, the cost of which is not much more than the permit only without the hassle. I suspect this is what the council want anyway, making more money with no work involved on their part which is why getting a permit is made so difficult.

We already delivered the kitchen units last week to be fitted in the basement. Today and tomorrow, we will be returning the remainder and unpacking all the boxes.

This is not something I usually recommend; packing is best done by the professionals but unpacking means putting everything back in the kitchen cupboards and in my experience is better done by the customer. As the insurance company is paying, they want us to do this however but may decide it wasn't such a good idea when they can't find where anything is in the morning for breakfast.

Saturday, 1ˢᵗ November 2008

This is not one of my better ideas, but when the work is slow, I am willing to try anything. There is a local market where I have hired a stall leading up to Christmas, the plan is to sell boxes and packing materials whilst raising the profile of our removals business.

Unfortunately, most people are just looking for a bargain present for Christmas and the last thing on their minds is moving house.

'What are you selling there?' An older, slightly deaf gentleman asks.

'My dignity,' I reply.

At the end of the day, Bob from the stall next to me buys five boxes and ten sheets of paper. I decided to give next Saturday a miss.

Tuesday, 11ᵗʰ November 2008

After delivering a customers' furniture from store yesterday, Dave and I have returned to re-assemble the wardrobes that had been dismantled. This is a job best done where there is plenty of space, as they are assembled lying down and then put in place; as well as allowing plenty of time which is why we have returned the following day. After a couple of hours, all is looking good until I realise one of the sections is facing the wrong way and has to be dismantled then re-assembled.

I recommend to the customer that they are fixed to the wall as all flat-pack furniture can be unstable, especially when sitting on the carpet; if there are children in the house, both chests of drawers and wardrobes have been known to fall on them causing harm.

Tuesday, 13th January 2009

An office move is welcome at this time of year as the housing market is not busy. This is only a small office but being on the second floor above high street shops makes it harder. There is no lift and some desks need to be dismantled to get them down the stairs. We are also parked on a yellow line although the traffic wardens are leaving us alone today. Maybe because it is a cold day, certainly the bacon rolls and tea from the local bakers' help keep the spirits up.

Monday, 8th June 2009

After delivering a few items to a house in the New Forest, the owner who has lived there many years tells me the best route to return home. I specifically ask him if the road is suitable for a truck as many are not in this part of the country. We follow his directions for two miles before arriving at a railway bridge, too low to drive under; this was why I didn't use the Sat Nav, thinking a local would know the best way.

As there is nowhere to turn around, the only option is reversing half a mile to the last junction we passed, avoiding motorists and local ponies on the way. It is a very wild and picturesque area to live in, although the beauty is lost on me at the moment.

Saturday, 13th June 2009

Situated half a mile from the Houses of Parliament, this top floor flat belongs to an elderly lady who has lived here for years. She is moving to a retirement village not far from Harrow. The new occupant being an MP buying it for the convenient location. I leave him a note about the pathetic system of buying and selling property that his government shows no interest in reforming.

Tuesday, 2nd August 2009

'Do you know Jeff Stelling?' Dave asks our customer who works for Sky Sports.

Although he knows who he is, presenting soccer Saturday every week, it is a bit like an American tourist asking if we know the Queen. Surprisingly, he does not know Jeff.

His family is moving near Portsmouth on the south coast with his youngest boy having a wardrobe in the shape of *Doctor Who's Tardis*. As we try to move the wardrobe up the stairs of the new house, it is apparent it will not fit around the bend in the stairs so has to be taken back down, dismantled and then re-assembled. I'm sure the doctor never had this problem.

Monday, 12th October 2009

Retirement homes can either be very helpful to the new person moving in or make our lives and theirs extremely difficult. The warden here falls in the second category as do the residents complaining about the door being left open while we are moving the new resident in.

Eventually, the only solution that satisfies everyone is for our eighty-year-old customer to sit by the front door to open and close it every time we are carrying furniture inside. After an hour in the cold, he starts to feel unwell and an ambulance has to be called to take him to the hospital. I despair at the lack of humanity and common sense shown by these petty-minded people.

Saturday, 17th October 2009

My son has been playing cricket at a local club in Harrow who are now moving from the park clubhouse to an old-fashioned cricket clubhouse a few miles away. Although still located in the same area, it is at the end of a narrow lane consisting of a wooden structure with viewing balconies that feels like it is in the country rather than a London borough.

The club secretary knows that I have a removal company so has asked me to move the cricket equipment for them. I am happy to help as some of the older players will be carrying the practice nets whilst others are dismantling the sight screens and loading the other assorted paraphernalia. All is going well until Tony appears carrying the giant scoreboard along with three others.

'It would have been helpful to have loaded that first,' I say.

Amateurs!

There is plenty of help however and we are soon driving to the new club house with the truck full.

'Can you collect a bar for us as well?' asks Shirley.

The next week when we have finished our job early, I take a diversion in to Central London to collect a bar that has been donated to the cricket club. It is dark by the time we arrive, but I'm sure this will be the most useful piece of equipment I have delivered for the parents at least.

Wednesday, 16th December 2009

'Merry Christmas,' I say.

Delivering bottles of wine to the estate agents and self-storage companies who have recommended our removals business during the last year.

I have learnt from previous experience that a little show of appreciation at this time of year goes a long way, although a cash gift is what most of the estate agents would prefer.

Wednesday, 6th January 2010

Snow fell heavily overnight and we arrive early at our yard to find everything is covered in a six-inch deep white blanket of snow. Driving to the job is hazardous as the roads are slippery. Sean has his window open looking for the road we are working in when a snowball flies through and hits him square in the face; a good shot by some passing kids but I don't think he is impressed.

Dave has parked his truck close behind a transit van while we are loading the Mercedes. He is unable to reverse it later that morning as the wheels keep spinning, so we have to dig the snow out from underneath the rear wheels then put old pieces of carpet down to provide traction. Finally, on our way to the new address, things are equally difficult there. John is sliding about all over and finding it impossible to stay on his feet. I suggest tomorrow he wears boots with a better grip as this weather is forecast to last all week.

Thursday, 7th January 2010

This is the busiest start to the year I have had in a long time and the weather is the heaviest snow we have had in years. We are trying to load one house today for a journey to the south coast tomorrow, at the same time moving a London underground employee locally in Harrow.

'Why have you got so many pairs of work boots?' I ask him.

'Because London underground issue new boots, jackets and trousers every three months,' he replies.

'No wonder the train fares keep going up then.'

Friday, 8th January 2010

Driving to the south coast with both trucks in convoy and heavy snow still on the ground, there is only one lane open on the dual carriageway as the other is thick with snow. The roads on the housing estate we are moving into are like a skating rink as all the snow has been compacted by traffic and turned to ice.

The journey each way takes twice as long as normal and when we arrive back at our yard it is dark, cold and late evening.

'You go home, lads, I'll put the trucks away.'

Easier said than done, as the yard is shared with two workshops and a coach company. Their vehicles have been in and out all day and turned the surface in to sheet ice. Every effort to reverse results in the rear wheels spinning and failing to move any distance on the slight incline.

The only solution is to lay a trail of carpet starting at the main gates all the way to our parking space, a distance of about 200 feet. After an hour of struggling, both trucks are finally parked up and I have made it to the end of the week. Snow really is much more fun when you are a kid. I expect I will enjoy tobogganing with my son down Harrow-on-the-hill much more this weekend.

Monday, 18th January 2010

There is still snow on the ground as we drive to the top of Harrow-on-the-hill to load this modern house built in the grounds of the old Kings Head pub. This pub used to be a real landmark as it dated back to Henry VIII's time. Now we slide the trucks in to the car park where there are just flats and houses built here.

This family are moving to Hampstead which is also on a hill, so I make sure we park downhill at both properties over the three days to avoid getting stuck in the snow again.

Thursday, 29th April 2010

Back again at this self-storage company, who have already recommended us several times this year already to their customers. It is always entertaining to watch people loading a small van and trying to fit more than is possible inside. The two men parked next to us at the moment are using the tailboard as an extension of the van to load that as well.

Apart from being unstable and unsafe, it is also overloaded with the weight of items, John and I are crying with laughter at the moment. I remember reading in our trade magazine about two heavily built men deciding to move themselves using a 3.5-tonne Luton van; after collecting the van, they were stopped at a weighbridge before having a chance to load anything, they were found to be overloaded just with their own bodyweight!

Friday, 28th May 2010

I am celebrating my birthday today by moving John's son and his wife from their first-floor maisonette into a nearby bungalow. John and his son, Chris, love football and he has a collection of programmes which fill a lot of heavy boxes. It is a pleasure seeing them so excited about moving into their new home with great plans to improve it for the future.

Thursday, 15th July 2010

Earlier this year, the volcanoes erupted in Iceland forming ash clouds and disrupting flights all over Europe. This is still on-going so Sheila, Kylam and I are driving to Dublin instead of flying and are on our way to Holyhead today to catch the ferry for Ireland. Sheila's niece, Marie, is marrying Tom this weekend and although it is a long drive at least we know we will get there, even if the Irish Sea is still a bit rough in the middle of summer.

Monday, 13th September 2010

The start of a four-day job, packing and moving a vicar to Wiltshire; John is packing his books all day which need to be kept in alphabetical order. I am delivering the first load today and although the house is in a new estate, there is a narrow drive lined with bushes to get to it. After much difficulty and a certain amount of trimming of the bushes, we are able to park by the front door making unloading the hundreds of book boxes much easier.

Again, there is a welcoming committee from the local community providing plenty of food and refreshment for us all.

Monday, 20th September 2010

This poor lady has been trying to move from her flat all summer and has had more than one promised removal date postponed. She is going to a retirement flat which is considerably smaller than her existing spacious one-bedroom property, and I am afraid she doesn't realise how much she has once we have packed everything.

Sitting on a chair as we fill every available space including the bathroom with boxes, she is looking more bemused by the minute and has nobody here to help. I can only comfort her and leave a pathway of boxes to her bed so she can at least sleep tonight and start fresh in the morning.

Thursday, 11th November 2010

A local estate agent has asked me to pack and move this house for storage as it is being re-possessed by the bank. I have collected the keys from the agent who is selling the property to an investor on behalf of the bank for a bargain price of £100,000.

The evicted family arrive at the self-storage unit as we are unloading to recover any clothes and personal items they may need until they can find somewhere to live. A very sad and too common situation at the moment.

Tuesday, 21st December 2010

Finishing the year as we started with more ice and snow, as I park outside this elderly man's house, I remember our problems in January and leave plenty of space to drive away later. He is sensibly disposing of all unnecessary furniture and effects which we take to the local dump on the way to his new flat. The charge for disposal is according to weight, which is a considerable cost as the council have increased their fees in recent years.

John and I finish unloading as the snowflakes start to fall again; we are just glad to get back in our yard without further difficulty.

2011 to 2015

Tuesday, 3rd February 2011

Having moved this family to Derby a few years ago so their son could fulfil his dreams of playing football for the local team. They are now moving back home which was sensibly rented out. It is a private estate that can only be accessed by driving over rough ground and through the local farmers' fields.

'There are midges everywhere,' Matthew says swatting them away from his face, 'you should have been here last time when we moved them in the summer.'

The "captain's chair" I use in my office was bought from this couple as the husband no longer used it and was therefore only collecting cobwebs in the shed.

Tuesday, 12th April 2011

The vicar of this church in Wembley has sold the surrounding land to a housing developer where they are busy building multiple homes. Part of the deal is to repair the church and build a new house for him and his family to live in. We, therefore, find ourselves in the middle of a building site carrying his furniture and boxes 50 feet from the old house to the new.

This is an unusual move, although I have delivered in the past to a flat in Ealing where the whole church was developed and complete with magnificent stain glass windows.

Monday, 8th August 2011

The family who returned from Derby earlier this year have now sold their home and are moving to Newbury, Wiltshire permanently. Their house has been hugely extended since they first bought it. The husband is a builder so internally it is completely different to the day they moved in when I was helping to rip up the carpet and sweep the floors before unloading the furniture. Some people leave their homes immaculately clean and tidy when they move out while others are less house proud.

Wednesday, 31st August 2011

Builders have bought this house along with several others on the main road as they want her garden space to build a small estate of houses. By knocking down one house and using all the other gardens, they plan to build 20 new homes in this development.

They are not so good at transferring the money though and leave our customer in a panic, thinking the move is not going to happen. There is a lot of dismantling with this job, even the sofas need the arms taking off, during which time the solicitors have had to make an amendment to the original contract and courier it over for the lady to sign.

As usual, everything is left until the last minute but finally the money arrives and she can move into her new bungalow.

Monday, 26th September 2011

My mum used to organise a ladies' group at her local church with this woman, who owns a house in a small village outside of Luton, now her husband has died and she wants to bring some items back to Harrow. It is an interesting cottage with the addition of an indoor swimming pool in a building at the bottom of the garden.

'We had some great parties here when the kids were young,' she tells me. Old cottages are always interesting, some I have been to come with gravestones in the garden, water wells or even rivers running underneath the home.

Tuesday, 4th October 2011

Sitting outside this house in Slough on an unusually warm day for early October, our customer comments:

'You may have to wait a while for the keys as the seller is very cautious and has instructed his solicitor not to release the keys until he is certain all is OK.'

This man used to own a toy shop in Harrow until ever-increasing rents forced him out.

'Fair enough,' I answer, leaning against the front door in the sunshine to eat my lunch.

As the door slowly opens from the pressure of my back, I think cautious he may be, but smart enough to lock the front door he is not, and we start to move in.

Friday, 7th October 2011

A friend of Darren and Alan in our yard also owns a coach company and wants to move from their house in Chiswick to a larger house in Ealing, a few miles away.

'You're parked a foot outside the parking bay,' a traffic warden tells me as I am walking out of the house.

'Piss off,' Darren's friend yells out the window,

'I've paid to have those bays suspended!'

The house they are moving into was owned by an elderly man who died, and his family have sold it as lived in which means a lot of building and renovation work needs to be done.

We move the basic furniture in and put the rest in to store, returning a few months later when the work is finished.

I discover from Darren that when the floorboards were lifted in the hall during renovation work, £10,000 in cash was found hidden by the previous owner, going some way towards paying for the work being done.

Friday, 28th October 2011

Divorce and moving house are equally stressful they say, so doing both at the same time is doubly, but it is also the reason a lot of people need to move home and this is one of those times.

We are using two separate trucks loading the husband's furniture on one and the wife's on the other; as the trucks turn in opposite directions at the top of the road, it feels symbolic of their lives at the moment.

Friday, 16th December 2011

Our last job before the Christmas shutdown which is starting early this year, as we begin to load, the snow starts to fall although this time I have brought a bag of salt to scatter over the path to keep it clear.

I remember my dad asking a customer once if they had any salt to put on the path. He was not impressed when they appeared at the front door carrying a salt and pepper pot!

Monday, 30th April 2012

Matthew has started working full time for me today. He is Dave's great-nephew (something like that) and has been helping out since he was 14 years old. He is a hard worker and good with manual tasks, so he will be a useful addition to our team. His first job will be a customer in Ealing who has been renting and storing while having extensive renovation work carried out on a house they bought six months ago.

They have been renting near to Ealing Film Studios so on our break, I have walked down the road to have a look, not much to see from the outside but these were iconic film studios in the 1960s, tucked away amid rows of terrace houses.

Monday, 23rd July 2012

A medical centre in Ruislip is having extensive building work and needs their patient files packed and stored in a metal shipping container that they have had placed in their car park for that purpose. The practice has to stay open during this time and needs to be able to access these files when required. It is therefore very important to keep them all in order and label the boxes carefully.

The practice manager has come to look for a sample file from the racks of boxes we have placed in the container, which I was pleased to see she found first time. What she doesn't realise is looking for a file in the warmth of summer is very different to searching on a cold winter's day in a metal box, since this work will not be completed before Christmas.

Saturday, 4th August 2012

The Olympics are in London and I was lucky enough to get tickets in the lottery draw for tonight's athletics, for what turned out to be super Saturday. Mo Farah, Jess Ennis and Greg Rutherford, all won gold medals this evening with an electric atmosphere in the crowd.

The noise and cheering were particularly loud when Mo Farah won the 10000km race with "Go Mo" echoing through the stadium and following him around the track like a wave of sound helping him to victory.

Monday, 13th August 2012

My mum is moving into a care home today and it is the saddest job I have ever had to carry out, a retirement flat at least still feels like a home but this feels more like a hospital room.

There is no truck needed here as her personal items fit in the back of my car and we try to make the room as homely as possible with a few pictures placed around. The staff are lovely and it is the best place for mum to be, but it is still very hard to walk away and leave her there.

Friday, 24th August 2012

As it is the school holidays, my son has come to work with us for a few days to "help", which consists of carrying a few boxes then climbing and jumping around the truck in between playing *Pokémon* on his Gameboy.

He misses the sleeper pod from our old Mercedes as he could climb up and down through the hole from the cab to the pod and look out the window up there on a journey.

I did get a strange look one day from a policeman who saw his legs dangling out the hole as we drove past him, but kept going before he could say anything.

Tuesday, 11th September 2012

'Didn't I move you here when you were younger?'

'Six years old to be exact,' the youngest son of the family replies.

He has driven from Cornwall yesterday to organise the removal and clearance of his late parents' home in Pinner. As his brother works abroad, he has been left with the job of organising everything for the family.

He wants to store some furniture for himself, some for his brother and send a truckload to the dump; so, we are in the middle of three days' work packing and moving.

I have left Matthew and John, the two apostles, at the home while I drive to the warehouse which is where I get a phone call from Matthew;

'We have accidentally set the panic alarm off in the bedroom while dismantling the bed,' is the first thing I hear before saying a word.

'Don't panic, I'll be there shortly,' I reply.

Arriving at the house half an hour later, they are both standing outside, waiting with the alarm still ringing but no-one else there. The son is out on other business. After speaking with him to get the alarm code, we are able to disarm it and carry on working.

Just as we are pulling out of the driveway a few hours later, two police cars with lights flashing and sirens going screech to a halt in front of the truck. I explain to the four policemen that either this is the slowest burglary in history or perhaps they should speak to the son by phone to confirm our identity. All is good and we can return the next day to finish the job.

Thursday, 4ᵗʰ October 2012

Devon is a popular county for people from London moving to this recent divorcee has sold the family home and is making a new start in the country. There is still all the kids' "stuff" to take as they will be staying with him some of the time.

The Sat Nav has taken us close to the property but is now telling me to drive down a narrow Devon lane to reach his house.

After stopping to phone the customer and discovering there is no mobile signal. I stupidly follow the nice lady on the Sat Nav's instructions and find myself in the middle of no-where with the lane, the same width as the truck. Finding anywhere to turn around is not easy, but after a few nerve-shredding miles, I manage a ten-point turn and head back.

The phone mast gods are briefly on our side, and I manage to contact the customer who can give me final directions to reach his home.

Wednesday, 28th November 2012

'Do you want a ticket for jumping a red light or not wearing a seatbelt?' the policewoman who has just appeared at my side window asks.

'Neither, as I didn't jump the light and don't need to wear a seatbelt,' is my reply. We were just driving through the centre of Brighton when I spotted a weirdly dressed woman walking along the street (not that unusual in Brighton),

'Look at her!' I cried, so John and Kylam (who had a day off school) lent forward to take a look, just as a police car was pulling out of the road opposite.

After following me for a mile, they turned the blue lights on then looked confused when finding no seatbelts in the cab for us to wear. Both in their early twenties, they called their sergeant for help who told them that yes, we should be wearing our non-existent seatbelts and to give us a ticket.

As this truck is currently 15 years old, there is no legal requirement for seatbelts to be fitted or worn, but there is an old adage that you can't argue with ignorance, especially when wearing a uniform, so I took the fine and moved on.

Thursday, 13th December 2012

My family and I are flying to Australia today to visit my brother, so we have closed early for Christmas and very excitedly driving to the airport. We won't have any snow to worry about this year.

Wednesday, 3rd April 2013

Currently in the process of selling mum's house to pay for her care home involved clearing a lot of furniture which is being collected by the RSPCA and the local hospice. I recommend both of these that whenever anyone has to give furniture away, they collect with their own vans and the money raised helps worthwhile charities.

I am also packing some boxes to send to my brother in Australia. Matthew and I will then take the remainder to the dump, an unpleasant job when it is your own family home. There is an old pram in the loft dating back to the 1960s which is covered in dust, but I would rather it was me clearing everything than a stranger.

Tuesday, 16th April 2013

The storage facility we were using is not as efficient as it used to be, so I have changed to a new warehouse in Northolt; this does mean moving our customers furniture between warehouses but it is better quality and will benefit everyone. As well as wooden storage boxes, there are large metal containers which are moved internally by crane-like something out of Pixar's Monsters Inc.

One of our customers has had her furniture in store for 14 years. I think if you haven't needed what is being stored in all that time, then you probably don't need it at all.

Tuesday, 14th May 2013

I have had to update the Mercedes truck to a newer vehicle to keep ahead of the London low emission zone regulations; this is a DAF truck which I am collecting from a trader in Kent working out of a farm. These places are always a bit chaotic run by a "Del Boy" lookalike which is why I arrange for my mechanic to check the vehicle over before driving it away.

Once back in our yard, it has to be adapted for removals by fitting a ramp to the rear and extra wooden bars to the inside for tying of furniture. This is something we can do ourselves using salvaged materials from previous vehicles, then once it is sign written, we will be ready to go.

Thursday, 6th June 2013

It's 7am and we are taking both trucks to the New Forest with a couple from Northolt, whose furniture we loaded yesterday, collecting some more items from a storage unit en route. As I approach the Southampton exit, a truck starts flashing me and honking his horn, repeated by another truck further along the road.

Pulling over in to a service road, Dave parks behind. We get out and see that the rear wheel nuts have come loose with half of them missing; this is causing the two rear tyres to wobble which is what the other truck drivers noticed.

One of the two tyres on the nearside was replaced when I bought the truck, obviously, the wheel nuts were not properly tightened and have worked loose over time.

It is not possible to repair the wheel now and we still have 20 miles to our destination, the only answer is to all get in the Ford truck and deliver that load, returning later to transfer the contents from one truck to the other and drive back to our customer's house.

By the time we got home, it is 11 pm with one truck still in Southampton; the next day my mechanic, Steve, drives with me to the DAF truck bringing a replacement wheel. The plan is to take the wheel to a local garage and swap the tyre from the old wheel to the new one. While waiting for the mechanic to finish, I get talking to the owner who is putting four tyres on a Ferrari which he tells me cost £10,000. They do work for the local showroom which recently had another Ferrari written off by a customer test driving it, making me feel better as we are able to fit the new tyre on the truck and drive home, cursing the Kent dealer all the way.

Thursday, 8th August 2013

The RAF used to limit their personnel to six tea chests when moving between bases, since this was a regular occurrence and paid for by them. Now they can move more, this man is taking furniture from his parents' home and storing it in his quarters at the RAF base in High Wycombe while he is posted abroad.

We have to report to security before entering the base and have our photos taken for entry passes, something John and Matthew want to keep as a souvenir.

I think they were expecting the inside to be more exciting and full of planes, but as this base is on top of a steep hill, it is only used for administrative purposes and one building is the same as the next.

As we were finished early, I decided to drive over to mum's care home which happens to be next to another RAF base in Northwood; on the way, I passed a council worker cutting the grass at the side of the road, suddenly the glass in my cars side window shattered where he had caught a stone and sent it flying through my window.

'Don't worry, mate, it happens all the time,' he said and arranged for their glass company to fix it the same day.

Thursday, 12th December 2013

The warning light started flashing, showing a faulty battery alternator as we returned from our job in Berkshire, but I kept driving, hoping it would wait until we got home. With 15 miles to go, the lights of the truck started to dim so I crossed my fingers and kept going until everything cut out and I had to park on the hard shoulder in the freezing cold of early evening.

The breakdown truck arrived a few hours later; the driver of this beast of a truck had been busy all day as I sat next to him in the cab he asked:

'How much do you think my boss just paid for this truck?'

'No idea,' I reply.

'£450,000,' he says.

'That's more than my house, no wonder he keeps you busy.'

As we approach our yard, I suddenly remember the low bridge which we will be too high for when hooked up to his truck and make a hasty diversion to avoid another disaster.

The drama is not over as the truck still needs to be manoeuvred in to our parking space in the yard. Bob, who is sleeping here at the moment (don't ask) comes out of his hut to see what is going on.

'The only way is to drop the truck close and push it the last bit,' the breakdown driver thinks. Bob looks very pleased with himself after saying,

'I just pushed a truck!' Using the last of the air in the brakes, I jump in the moving vehicle and bring it to a halt before it demolishes our office.

Monday, 6ᵗʰ January 2014

The government have introduced a new test for anyone driving an HGV or coach called the Certificate of Professional Competence or CPC for short. This entails a weeks' course in a classroom setting reminding professional drivers how to drive safely; a good idea in theory but 35 hours compulsory attendance could have been covered in one day at considerably less time and money.

There is a real mix of people of all ages and backgrounds, looking bleary-eyed at the 7am starting time. By the end of the day, they are just struggling to keep their eyes open.

The tipper drivers are in for a real shock as part of their training involves cycling around London to improve awareness of vulnerable road users such as cyclists; as they are the most overweight group, I hope London ambulance service have been put on standby.

Friday, 21ˢᵗ February 2014

Not only does this elderly man have a lot of books and a piano, he is struggling to reduce the furniture he needs when downsizing to a smaller property. We have had to use both our trucks and are now finding it difficult to reverse either of them up the long drive.

To avoid the extra time and effort carrying everything up, the slope I am trying to reverse the DAF truck when the mud flap becomes caught under the rear wheels bending the metal bar supporting it.

This is when our trollies are a god send, especially for the piano, but the unloading is a lot longer and harder work than I had expected.

Thursday, 24th April 2014

Looking out over Dover harbour in Kent is this property with an amazing view. Our customer was storing his belongings in a self-storage unit which we loaded yesterday for delivery today. He is a bit of a character for an older man, driving a soft top jeep and moving in to this modern home set over three floors, I just hope he keeps his mobility as good as it is now.

The motorway leading to Dover must have the most HGV's in the country with the town itself, constantly busy day and night; there is a telescope set in the house to watch the ferries come in and out of the harbour, as well as anyone escaping from the back of the trucks.

Wednesday, 28th May 2014

The specialist company I get to move awkward pianos are helping again today with a grand piano which is this lady's pride and joy, belonging as it did to her late husband. They are delivering it to our warehouse where we will meet them with the rest of the load later, having delivered a few items on the way. We will then be loading from store the container for tomorrow's delivery to Bristol.

Thursday, 29th May 2014

This house is in the old part of Bristol near the cathedral and is a beautiful 18th century property set over five floors. The lady moving in is joining her extended family who are all West Indian in origin, which is ironic as she tells me this house was originally built for a wealthy slave trader.

Each room has a beautiful fireplace with cornicing and decorated ceilings, although I am glad to say after the guided tour of the house, most of her furniture is in the basement or ground floor.

Thursday, 10th July 2014

Our couple have a young child and are moving from a first floor flat to a house. We already moved the lady out on Tuesday; there is a long walk to the stairs and no lift so I can see why they are moving with a young child. This is why we started packing and loading yesterday.

As we are unloading in to the new house, her next-door neighbour's daughter comes running outside to say her dad has fallen out of his chair and can we help lift him off the floor.

He may be frail but is also a dead weight and it takes two of us to lift him. I notice his kitchen only has a sink and a standpipe with no modern appliances; apparently, he has lived here over 50 years.

Monday, 14th July 2014

My son, Kylam, is starting a week's work experience with Anthony, who works in our yard for Darren, renting vans and cars to the public. This is a new addition to the coach company and I asked them if they would let him help them out for the week as part of his school curriculum.

From what I see coming in and out of the yard, his work experience mostly consists of eating takeaway pizza and winding up Alan, Darren's dad. They are nice people though and as Anthony say:

'He'll get to see how shit work is.'

Tuesday, 7th August 2014

I am meeting our customer today at the warehouse; we stored his late parent's furniture for him and his brother last year. We are helping to load the items they want to keep on to the separate vans they have hired, then putting the remainder on our truck for delivery to an Auction house in Amersham tomorrow.

I am packing their vans as well as my own, especially the brother who has to drive all the way back to Cornwall, some of the mirrors and furniture are very delicate. There are some vintage clothes we are also taking to auction for another customer, and the owner is more interested in these than the antique furniture as a lot of their regular clients will be bidding.

Wednesday, 10th September 2014

This news agent in Rayners Lane has been here since I was a kid. I remember buying bottles of fizzy drink here when you still got money back for returning the empty bottle. The old couple have sold up and are putting everything in to storage while waiting for their home on the south coast to be ready.

Everything has to be loaded out the back of the shop down awkward narrow stairs, carrying furniture past yellow nicotine-stained paintwork and walls from years of smoking.

When all has been loaded and stored in the warehouse, there is still time to put a small job from store on the truck for delivery tomorrow. This is for a man who used to be a car dealer in Harrow, selling a few cars to my dad in his time, who is now moving to a retirement home in Pinner.

Thursday, 18th December 2014

The first thing I notice as we arrive outside the house to continue loading from yesterday is the wardrobe half in and half out of the top floor window. Our customer's son is helping his dad and with a little help from ourselves, the wardrobe makes it to the ground floor.

It is a short drive to the town in Bedfordshire but we finish late due to the usual wait for keys. I had planned to visit my mum in her home when finished but it will have to wait, sadly she dies early tomorrow morning.

Friday, 20th February 2015

As John and I walked out of the house, we are currently unloading in; I notice an elderly man parked 20 yards in front of our truck, examining the front of his car. We are parked on a main road in Somerset which is not busy and with plenty of room for two cars to pass;

'Are you alright,' I shout out.

I can see the front nearside of his small car is badly damaged with broken glass and a door mirror hanging off, the elderly man is looking a bit shaken.

He has clipped the back of our stationary truck while attempting to overtake, causing all this damage; when I look at the rear of our vehicle expecting to see major damage, there is only a slight scrape in the paintwork visible. Maybe it is time he reviews his driving licence; I won't be making the day any worse by claiming on his car insurance.

Monday, 23rd February 2015

The Ford truck needs to be sold as it will no longer meet current emission standards for London. I am waiting for a buyer to meet me at the yard when I get a phone call from my son's school to say he is being taken to hospital by ambulance and can I meet him at the school now.

Anthony and Darren take over the sale for me and I arrive at the same time as the ambulance;

'We were just talking about your son when we got this call,' comments the ambulance driver, since they collected him with a pneumothorax a few weeks ago which has re-occurred.

My wife meets us at the hospital from work. Kylam now has to have an operation to fix his lung permanently which is a worrying time for everyone.

Friday, 27th February 2015

Work still has to carry on, so we arrive at this house in Buckinghamshire having driven past the front entrance twice looking for the way in. There are a few houses hidden away behind an electric wooden gate on the main road, our truck only just fits through the opening but there is then a steep driveway to our property which the rear of the DAF cannot negotiate without "bottoming out".

This is when the overhang at the back of the vehicle hits the ground before the wheels can raise it high enough. Fortunately, not a common problem but the result here is carrying everything a considerable distance uphill using trollies or by hand.

After finishing, there is still time for a hospital visit putting our problems into perspective.

Thursday, 26th March 2015

'You're early, we haven't finished yet!' shouts the painter as I approach the front door.

This is a new development of houses near Nottingham and we are indeed half an hour earlier than agreed with our client as to the time we would meet him here.

As he is still painting the front door and internal banisters, I don't think the extra half hour would have made much difference, especially as we now have to unload ensuring wet paint does not touch any of the furniture or ourselves.

Another builder who likes to leave everything until the last minute on moving in day before finishing all the jobs, at least the wooden floor had been laid.

Tuesday, 30th June 2015

A friend of my brothers from his Rugby playing days is moving to Norfolk, having stored their furniture while building work was carried out in their new house.

The builders are busy at work when we arrive on a very hot summers day. The first job is to clear their van, tools and equipment out of the way so we can get access to the property.

I understand not wanting to pay storage for any longer than is necessary, it is a trade-off with delivering your belongings into an on-going building site.

Thursday, 20th August 2015

Dave is no longer working and has cleared out his family home to move in to a retirement flat in Harrow; everything is packed and ready to go, as I would expect from someone involved in removals most of his life.

When he started working packing involved tea chests with the glass and china wrapped in newspaper; as the print came off the papers then, everything had to be washed after being unpacked.

Friday, 4th September 2015

My mechanic Steve is fitting a forward-facing mirror to the DAF today as this is now compulsory along with the five other mirrors. Amazingly, there have been accidents, even recently, when the truck driver has not been aware of a car facing sideways across the front of the truck and continued driving pushing the car along the motorway.

The most recent occasion was a Royal Mail truck pushing a car unaware on the M40 before the singer Ellie Goulding and her driver flagged him down and stopped to help, presumably offering a change of underwear.

Monday, 26th October 2015

This couple is moving from their temporary flat into a relatively new development in Ruislip with amazing views over London.

After finishing delivery, they take us up to the roof on the 15th floor where the view is even more spectacular with tables and chairs available for the residents to relax in.

The only downside is the wind, even on a calm day like today, it is still blowing at quite a strength. I hope the tables and chairs are well secured.

Friday, 12th December 2015

Since Anthony has been renting vans out of our yard, there has been no need to replace the truck I sold earlier in the year; we are using one of his smaller vans today which I am driving.

There is a speed limiter fitted which I have accidentally turned on while changing gear, the switch being next to the gearstick and am now wondering why I cannot drive faster than 25mph.

After phoning Anthony, who is not able to help over the phone, I work out the problem and do not have to drive all the way to Suffolk in third gear.

2016 to 2020

Tuesday, 1ˢᵗ March 2016

The tendons in both my arms have been hurting for a few months so I have an appointment today with a physio at Sheila's place of work. As well as massaging the muscles, he suggests acupuncture and produces the biggest needles I have ever seen. After he accidentally touches a nerve, I decide to follow my brother's advice:

'My physio suggested acupuncture as well,' he said.

'What did you do?'

'Changed my physio,' was his reply.

Thursday, 24ᵗʰ March 2016

We are flying to Hong Kong tomorrow to visit my brother who has been living and working there for the past year; todays removal is the mother of a previous customer who is moving to a retirement village just outside of London.

There have been a lot of people moving recently since the government decided to change the tax on buy to let properties at the end of the month, creating a rush to beat the deadline.

I agreed to do this last job before closing for the early Easter break, however, the solicitors keep us all waiting until

4 pm before the elderly lady can relax and finally move into her new home.

These villages are becoming more popular as there is a lot of social activity including a bar and restaurant in the main building, giving both independence and peace of mind at the same time.

Monday, 11th April 2016

I delayed moving this family from store while I was away, giving them time to finish renovations to their new house. One feature they have kept is an indoor swimming pool attached to the lounge and accessed through sliding doors which then led to a bedroom on the other side.

It is a very unusual layout, although I am sure the young children will get plenty of use from it as will the husband with his full-size snooker table in the basement. I have seen all sorts with sunken baths in the bedroom alongside mirrored ceilings over the bed, but usually, indoor pools are in a separate area of the house.

Monday, 25th April 2016

A piano teacher who has lived in the same road for over 30 years is always going to know a lot of people, some of her past and present pupils have called around to say goodbye while we are moving her to Reading.

The piano is obviously an important part of the move for her and has to be lifted on its end using the piano wheels to exit the room she taught from. I am glad when it is safely positioned in the new property where she is able to play a melody to prove all is well. If re-tuning is all that is needed, the customer should be satisfied.

Friday, 24th June 2016

'I am so upset that we are leaving Europe,' bemoans this lady. Currently visiting her house the day after the referendum vote, she is showing me around the property so I can quote for her upcoming move to store and then Oxford.

It is fairly obvious which way she voted with the family also owning a house in the south of France; later in the year, we move them to a lovely home overlooking the river Thames in Oxford, not quite the riviera but beautiful views all the same.

Friday, 26th August 2016

Murphy's law says that when the solicitor manages to transfer the money between banks on time, the person moving out of the house will be late emptying their belongings. This is the case today, and even by mid-afternoon, there is still a considerable amount outside the property to move.

We begin to unload while the previous occupants are still loading; John decides to open the double-glazed bedroom window as it is a hot day, and the next thing Matthew and I see is the window flying through the air narrowly missing us on the front footpath before embedding itself in the lawn.

'All I did was push the window open,' exclaims John.

At least nobody is hurt, we secure the window back in and advise our customer to check all the others carefully at a later date.

Wednesday, 31ˢᵗ August 2016

As our customer already owns their new house, I have decided to move their outside pot plants in advance of the main removal; there are over 200 various shapes and sizes to go from the garden. Most can be transported using trollies but the largest and heaviest require lifting over next doors fence to exit through their larger side gate.

A particularly large houseplant needs some pruning to fit through the internal doors of both houses, finally the truck is full of plants resembling an exhibition at Kew gardens. Twenty-five years ago when I started working with my dad, people rarely took plants from their garden, foreign holidays have a lot to answer for.

Monday, 17ᵗʰ October 2016

Our friends have bought a cottage in a small village while living abroad and need some help collecting furniture they have stored in Hereford and Devon. I am using my truck to move the bulk of the items stored with Kate's family in Hereford, but we are delayed by a major road accident before even reaching Oxford.

Not arriving at the cottage until late in the day, which Kate hasn't seen properly until this point, there is a problem parking without blocking the only road into the village. Our first job is to get the heating working, then the moment we park to unload, everyone in the village including the local farmer in his tractor decide they have to drive past now but somehow we make it work.

The following day I have hired a van from Anthony for the drive down to Devon where the remainder of their belongings are stored on a farm. The roads are narrow, and in some cases extremely steep, which is why I am using a smaller vehicle; the farm is exactly as you would imagine a typical farm to be, old barns with a traditional farmhouse and a very hospitable farmers wife.

Saturday, 29th October 2016

We moved this elderly couple into a retirement home earlier in the year; unfortunately, the husband does not like it so they are going back to the original house they were living in. The flat was more suitable for his wife, but he found it impossible to settle in the home and missed his house he had lived in most of their lives.

Their daughter is very patient and understanding; it is not easy doing the right thing for your parents when they reach a certain age.

Thursday, 12th January 2017

The daughter of our customer is taking a photo of our truck as we are loading her parents' furniture, a memory of the day they moved from her family home, especially as their surname is the same as mine.

It has just started to snow when we arrive at their bungalow. Part of a retirement village, I have moved many people to before, so to protect their carpet we lay protection all over the floor. Our piano wheels prove invaluable once again; we may only move half a dozen pianos each year but it would be extremely difficult without the correct equipment.

It is dark outside as we leave for home; there is a white carpet of snow covering the ground as well as all the trees and vehicles creating a magical wonderland.

Thursday, 14th March 2017

Located beside our yard, this house has not been touched for years and the person living here is a hoarder who is finding it very difficult to get rid of anything. Matthew and I were here yesterday part-loading, now John is back from holiday driving the additional Luton van I have hired from Anthony; both trucks are full of boxes containing clutter that will never be used.

Arriving at the new house, I am horrified to see it is not only half the size of the old one but also at the end of a long uphill path from the road. We are all exhausted at the finish leaving the customer surrounded by boxes, most of which will never be opened.

Friday, 23rd June 2017

'I was lucky to sell this house,' our customer comments as we enter the room.

He goes on to explain how the council discovered a disused mine under the junior school opposite after a hole appeared in the staff car park and that the tunnel runs under the road to the edge of his property.

This should have been a sign that this would be a difficult move; their new home is at the top of a steep hill in Bridport, Dorset and on a hot summers day we are once again greeted with a long walk from the end of the road down a winding path to the front gate.

After six hours unloading in the heat of the day, we are finally finished just as it is starting to cool down, and John is getting cramp in his legs. He decides soon after that it is time to give his body a rest and take early retirement, having been a loyal and hard-working colleague for many years.

Friday, 7th July 2017

Driving to East London along the western avenue takes us past Grenfell Tower, the scene of a horrendous fire three weeks ago resulting in many deaths. It is just charred wreckage now standing tall amidst surrounding tower blocks like a burnt match in an otherwise unused box of matches.

As Matthew and I arrive at our own customers' block of flats, it is a reminder of how many people live in rundown tower blocks in Central London. The flat itself is quite nice with a view over the city of London business sector, a world away from the flats we are currently in with ancient lifts and dark stone corridors.

Thursday, 26th September 2017

My grandmother used to live in these council flats; most are now privately owned and our client has left us alone to pack and load their furniture for delivery to store.

Kylam is helping Matthew and I, having recently come out of hospital he is building his strength by doing removals. There is a long walk to where our truck is parked; it shows his mental and physical toughness that he is able to keep working throughout the day.

Friday, 27th October 2017

I used to play tennis with this lady at our local club in North Harrow. She is now moving to a small village in Northamptonshire to be close to her sister.

The cottage is 200 years old with some of the doors only five feet tall which is fine for Julie as she is short in stature but is not so good for Kylam who is six feet seven.

We are all nursing bumps to our heads on finishing, but working has helped his fitness before flying to America tomorrow to follow his dream of playing basketball.

Friday, 24th November 2017

'What happened to your face?' I ask our customer as he opens the door.

'I was mugged,' is his reply.

We have been loading this second floor flat with no lift since yesterday and have returned to finish the job to be greeted by our customer sporting a black eye. He is a baker by trade and was returning home late last night when he was attacked getting out of his car.

Along with his wife, they are a lovely couple even helping to carry some of the lighter boxes downstairs; the excitement of moving in to their first house together soon trumps any worries from last night if anything confirming the reason for wanting to move.

Tuesday, 19th December 2017

There is ice on the road and pavement outside this old lady's house, so our first job is to clear a path so we are not sliding about too much. The daughter is helping her mum as she has lived here for over 50 years but is sensibly only taking what she really needs and giving the rest to charity.

Her mum has an oven and a fridge that are both older than I am, which are kept in immaculate condition as is the rest of the home. A lot of people from this generation take a pride in keeping their home and contents in good order; it is a pleasure to take the stress out of the moving process for them.

Friday, 5th January 2018

Our first removal of the New Year has my son Kylam working with us full time having just returned from America. My dad's prediction of fourth-generation Willis Removals has come true if only for the short term. I will be able to give him some all-round work experience to help with his future career prospects.

This Indian lady is moving mostly boxes from her parents' house to her own home in Northwood. I have taken this job on from her list of items sent by email and as is often the case, she has been economical with the truth regarding the number of boxes to be moved.

She clearly has no intention of paying any more money so we are also economical with the number of heavy boxes carried upstairs, leaving her with a very full downstairs living room.

Monday, 12th February 2018

This lady is moving back to her own home with her children after staying with her parents temporarily to get financially back on her feet. As we are loading and dismantling furniture, they are packing the last items and looking for the family cat who has disappeared.

This is not unusual as all cats hate moving and as this is the parent's home; there is no urgency to find her so we get on our way.

At the new address the first thing I hear on opening the back of the truck is a "meow", the cat having hidden among the boxes now climbs deeper inside for safety.

'Don't worry,' our customer says, 'she grew up here so won't get lost.'

As we unload further into the truck, the black and white cat also moves further until there is nowhere left to hide and she makes a run for it.

Leaping off the back after avoiding our lunging arms, she disappears into the distance until later being spotted creeping back up the road; I made sure the back was completely empty before driving away.

A friend of mine who works for an International Removal Company once brought a cat-back accidentally from France with the customer's furniture being moved to London; as the cat emerged from the truck, it was recognised as belonging to the ex-neighbour of their client, so arrangements had to be made to ship the cat back home at considerable expense.

Tuesday, 20th February 2018

I am delivering this lady's furniture which has been in storage for 14 years; there is a piano which has to be carried to the first floor of the maisonette together with assorted furniture and boxes.

She is a lovely person but again finds it difficult to dispose of anything. The maisonette already being full makes it hard to find space for the items we are delivering.

Her mum died recently and had lived with her the last 14 years, meaning these aren't just belongings but memories of their life together.

Friday, 2nd March 2018

The beast from the east, the weathermen call this week of snow with temperatures barely getting above freezing during the day. We are driving to a flat in St Albans to bring an elderly lady back to a retirement home in Pinner; the first job is to clear the snow and ice using the salt and grit left outside.

The lady is bringing far too much for a small retirement flat and as there is a long walk to her door, loading takes some considerable time.

After waiting for the keys, we finally get started—having lost most of the feeling in our fingers and toes. Just as the snow starts to fall heavily again, Kylam can't resist attacking Matthew with snowballs whenever he is not looking, but we finally get finished and go home where my first job is to thaw out the frozen boiler pipes to get the heating working again.

Friday, 9th March 2018

The snow has thawed which is just as well since we find ourselves walking up a fire escape and over a flat roof to reach the rear entrance of this bar in Harrow.

'What's that smell?' the lads ask.

'Stale beer and cigarettes,' I reply.

It's a familiar smell with most pub accommodation, ashtrays overflowing and half-empty pint glasses are usually left lying about. We are moving the landlord's personal belongings to his new pub in Southampton, having hired a small van from Anthony.

The locals are interested to see who the new landlord will be; he is a tough Scotsman who won't take any rubbish, but I think he will find it a lot quieter than he is used to.

Saturday, 17th March 2018

The cold weather is unrelenting and we are moving an Indian family to Beaconsfield just outside of London where they have been renovating a house for six months. Even though I have reversed the truck up their driveway, it is still icy on the front step which keeps re-freezing due to the cold.

There is an American fridge freezer which has to be unplumbed together with the fridge doors having to be removed to fit out of the kitchen; Matthew is expert at this and equally good at re-assembling later.

The snow has started to fall as we arrive at the new house where the builders are frantically trying to finish the work so the family can sleep here tonight; as long as the heating is working, they will be alright.

Monday, 26th March 2018

After packing and loading this couple on Saturday, we are on our way to Gloucestershire, passing through the Cotswolds and then Cheltenham when I hear a bang.

'What was that!' I cry out, before realising the steering is heavy.

'A flat tyre.'

We have a breakdown service but they are only able to offer a tow to the nearest garage, it is quicker to contact a local tyre firm to come to us with a replacement tyre.

After an hour, a helpful man arrives and replaces the tyre so we can continue on our journey, thankfully it happened in town and not on the Cotswold country road we had just driven along.

Wednesday, 18th April 2018

'Can you move us out of our house today?' this lady pleads on the phone.

They had planned to live in their house while having extensive building work but have reached the point where the noise, dust and general disruption is overwhelming and want to move out as soon as possible.

We are packing and loading today to take to store tomorrow; there is some valuable furniture and electrical equipment this couple is particularly worried about moving, although they were not bothered about leaving it in what is now a building site.

Once my counselling skills are put to good use, they both calm down, had they planned things better it would not be so stressful for everyone, and my head would not be bleeding from hitting it on the scaffolding.

Wednesday, 2nd May 2018

'My husband and I have lived here 65 years,' our customer says.

They are having their wooden floor polished and need some antique furniture moved into the garage to make space, not as easy as it sounds as some of it is very heavy and needs dismantling.

After finishing here, we go to the university campus in Harrow where an Egyptian student wants to store a few boxes of personal belongings before returning home for the summer, two very different clients in the same day.

Thursday, 31st May 2018

A regular customer needs her leather sofas moved from one first floor maisonette to another. As I had moved her in a few years ago, I remember how heavy and awkward these were. They are equally difficult to get into her new home as they were coming out of the existing one; it's a good thing she is a nice lady and her family regular customers.

I then drive to the home of another family friend of my parents like a lot of people their age. His wife is no longer able to use the stairs even with a stair lift. We have called around to move some bedroom furniture downstairs to make life easier for them, the least I can do to help out.

Thursday, 14th June 2018

"I think we are going to need a locksmith" are not the words you want to hear when moving home.

The son of the elderly lady we are moving to a retirement home has accidentally left the house keys inside when closing the door; this would not matter except for:

[a] They are the only set of keys.

[b] We have agreed to return some furniture from her new flat back to her old home.

After finishing the removal to her new flat, we have returned to the house and are waiting for the locksmith to arrive. It takes him two minutes to enter the property and the slightly red-faced son can now relax.

Thursday, 5th July 2018

After a cold winter, this is becoming a hot summer, not ideal when inside packing a mountain of books and magazines in to boxes.

'This guy has got some weird shit,' is the reaction as we pack black magic and religious cult magazines from the spare bedroom.

In the past I have found a variety of sex aids, adult magazines and also discovered £1000 hidden under the mattress; the customer being delighted when I handed them the money back, although I'm not so sure about the other items.

We are delivering this to Suffolk tomorrow where once again we are kept waiting by both the solicitor and customer collecting the keys, so don't get back home until 9 pm.

Thursday, 27th September 2018

Today the DAF truck is acting up again with a fuel problem my mechanic seems unable to fix; having changed all the relatively inexpensive parts over the last month. While I am contemplating the option of spending more money with no guarantees or changing the vehicle, there is the loudest thunderclap from outside the house we are unloading in to.

Seconds later there is a lightning strike a few hundred yards from where we are parked, knocking out all the electrics in the road. Much closer and I wouldn't have to worry about the truck, the thunderstorm that follows is of biblical proportions and we spend the next half hour sheltering inside along with a very frightened dog.

Saturday, 20th October 2018

I have decided to upgrade the truck as there are new emission controls in two years when I will have to change it anyway; collecting the Mercedes today from the dealer, it takes a while to get used to driving a different vehicle, especially as this is the first time using a semi-automatic gearbox.

My dad was thrilled the first time he experienced power steering in a truck, previously having had to stand up in the cab to try to slowly turn the wheel when parking, even having men pushing the tyre at the same time to help.

I have had to go on YouTube so I can work out how to use the semi-automatic gearbox correctly, something I thought I would never say I needed to do.

I just need to load an array of equipment including trollies, toolbox, blankets, ties, tape and boxes before we can use the Mercedes for removal on Monday.

Tuesday, 30th October 2018

This family are moving from a two-bedroom maisonette because they have outgrown the space, looking at our truck when loaded you would expect them to have come from a four-bedroom house. They are moving less than a mile so we arrive at the new house by 1 pm and wait; at 5 pm, we are still waiting and it has got dark.

Our customer finally receives a phone call from the solicitor at 5.30 pm to say the money has not been transferred into the vendors account, even though the sale of their property has already happened. We will have to wait until tomorrow when hopefully the banks and solicitors will get their act together, it is too late now as they have all gone home.

Fortunately, the truck is not booked for a removal tomorrow; we are therefore able to return and finally move this family in to their new home.

Wednesday, 7th November 2018

This lady was suffering from dementia when we moved her earlier this year; we have now returned to her old home as her son wants the remainder of the belongings taken and stored at his garage in Essex.

His house is down a single-track lane and the Sat Nav directs us the wrong way, two miles along a narrow track and I am praying we don't meet another vehicle coming the other way.

Unsuitable for large vehicles, the sign reads before we finally reach the entrance to his property, a large house set in five acres of ground.

He could start his own storage business here since there is a choice of garages and barns with pheasants roaming freely and stables out the back. I know the lads want to have a ride on the horses, unfortunately, these and the quad bikes are off-limits.

Thursday, 13th December 2018

Last month we were moving a customer from the downstairs maisonette to the upstairs of the same property; today it is moving to the house next door as well as loading plants to take to the New Forest. The back of the truck again looks like a nursery, one of the plants being too big to even stand upright and has to be tied at an angle to fit.

The customer's new home is in the heart of the New Forest; wild ponies are grazing on the other side of the fence, and we have to be careful they don't wander into the garden. Arranging the large climbing wisteria around the back door and distributing the other plants around the patio, perhaps I should change careers to landscape gardening in future.

Thursday, 31st January 2019

'The forecast is for heavy snow this evening,' the weatherman says as we are driving along the M4 motorway to Bath.

I have hired a transit van so we can get there and back quickly (hopefully before the snow arrives) and because parking is extremely difficult at the flat we are moving into.

The only place to stop on the main road into Bath is on a nearby driveway where we quickly off-load the van into the front garden before parking elsewhere. The flat is the top floor of a converted Georgian house with a beautiful frontal façade but all the internal features sadly ripped out.

There are 50 steps to climb before reaching the front door, so with aching knees we make it back to London a couple of hours before the snow starts to fall, closing the M4 motorway by the next morning.

Tuesday, 19ᵗʰ February 2019

The renovation works for this house were scheduled to take six months but instead took nearly a year. This is the final delivery of boxes including the husband's collection of empty beer cans.

I have seen some weird collections over the years, usually, I have to say by men; Star Wars memorabilia is popular as are beer cans/ bottles. There have also been collections of sewing machines dating back 100 years as well as garden gnomes, the most unusual however being a garden covered in full-size red letterboxes from the 20th century.

The long-suffering wife is usually hoping their husband will get rid of the collection before moving; in my experience, he is usually not bothered about the furniture as long as his pride and joy arrives undamaged.

Wednesday, 7ᵗʰ August 2019

While Matthew is on holiday, Kylam and I are working at a dentist's where the owner has retired and is taking his remaining equipment to be stored at his home in Chertsey. The dentist chairs can be sold as they are popular with tattoo artists and the remaining cabinets, tools and files are stored in his garage for future use; this would have been my dad's worst nightmare as he hated a visit to the dentist or anything to do with them.

Returning to London in the afternoon, Kylam receives a phone call from some friends asking for help to jump-start their car, so we head off with some jump leads from our office to save the day.

They have been trying to push start the car by going up and down the car park turning the ignition key without realising it has to first be in gear.

A quick lesson on where to place the leads and how to push start in the future and they are on their way, ready for the next time there is a flat battery.

Friday, 16th August 2019

'It went up the stairs so it must come down,' the lady comments.

How often have I heard this said when someone has forced a piece of furniture up the stairs or altered the layout by fitting a loft extension and thereby reducing the space available.

This particular wardrobe will not fit down the stairs due to a large radiator being fitted since it was moved in; dismantling it is the only option which is an interesting challenge as it has never been taken apart before.

It is that sort of a day as their new build house has a space left in the kitchen for the washing machine to fit in to, but the builders have fitted a radiator there making the gap now too small.

Friday, 4th October 2019

Some new build properties are built to a very high standard, as with this one in Denham where the bathroom fittings are futuristic and his mobile phone controls all electrical and heating appliances.

Slightly less high tech is the pipework from our truck that the mechanic has removed this afternoon, and I have now taken to a specialist engineer for a copy to be made. The workshop is located on a large industrial estate where I assume there must be a good transport café nearby to have something to eat while waiting.

'Do you have any meat?' I ask looking at the menu board.

'This is a vegan café,' replies the owner.

I wish you luck; with that I think to myself, having to settle for a vegetarian wrap instead of the sausage sandwich I was craving.

Friday, 15th November 2019

This is the second marriage for our customer having building work carried out on the home that her new husband has recently joined her in, which I originally moved her into several years ago.

At that time, her first husband had recently died and one of her most treasured possessions was the vase sitting on a bookshelf; as I was packing, she told me to take great care of that since her husband's ashes were inside.

Despite secretly looking around, I cannot see any sign of the vase now, probably best not to mention it to her new husband.

Monday, 2nd December 2019

Matthew's brother, Ryan, is with us on work experience from his college this week. The first day must seem to him like we work in a madhouse. This eighty-year-old widow is moving out of the only home she shared with her husband since marrying him in her 20s. It is understandably an emotional day and there are lots of tears and tantrums along the way, her sister is trying to help but the move is chaotic to say the least.

Every item has an emotional attachment but they cannot all fit into her new retirement flat; Ryan is looking increasingly confused as I try to mediate between the two sisters, probably wondering what the rest of the week will entail.

Eventually, we arrive at the new flat only to be left waiting in the cold (the two sisters included) until 5 pm when the keys are finally released for us to unload in time for bed.

Thursday, 19th December 2019

Having started this move by packing on Monday, we are finally able to deliver this elderly widower's furniture to his bungalow in Norfolk. Once again there was a delay with the money being transferred on time between the solicitors and banks with each one blaming the other.

The result was holding his furniture for two days on the truck until the dispute was resolved, something that should have been done a long time before the day of the removal.

Friday, 24th January 2020

At the start of my 30th year working in furniture removals, I have calculated the distance walked carrying customer's furniture to be the equivalent of walking twice around the world.

Today's client has been recommended to us like so many others over the years and has a young family he is moving to a larger rented family home.

As both properties are nearby and we already have the keys, it makes sense to move over two days with the family not sleeping in their new home before Monday. This proves to be fortunate as the heating is not working when we deliver the first load today; the estate agent cannot be bothered to sort the problem so it is left to the customer and ourselves to get the boiler working and some heat in the house.

After much head-scratching, Matthew gets the gas turned on and the boiler running before the rest of the family arrive; the letting agent still not being in contact.

Monday, 3rd February 2020

This is another regular customer whose family I have moved a few times. His two sons have bought a brand new flat in central Harrow and need some furniture and personal belongings transported.

As with most new flats, the lift will only allow you to use them with a key fob like with all hotels now; our customer tells me his boss was once trapped in their office lift from Friday evening until Monday morning, not something you want to hear when travelling up to the fifth floor.

On returning to our yard, I am greeted by a strange-looking man who has been phoning me all morning; he wants to move to Manchester as soon as possible; telling me he has recently married an illegal immigrant who stole his money before throwing him out of his house.

Suspecting he might be a sandwich short of a picnic, I usher him into our office where he confirms he is on day release from Northwick Park hospital, also saying that our yard is dangerous and that he used to be a health and safety executive.

'I would worry more about your own problems,' I said, pushing him out of the door as quickly and safely as possible.

Friday, 6th March 2020

This brother and sister have sold the family home to live together by the sea in Norfolk. They had wanted to move in today but I convinced them it would be better to wait until tomorrow when they have the keys in their hand.

When they arrived at the bungalow which had been sold by probate, this very tidy pair was shocked to find the property left in a complete mess.

They spent all night and next morning cleaning, the brother telling me his stomach was knotted with worry all night thinking they had done the wrong thing.

After a little counselling and organising of their belongings to make it look homely, they had both calmed down and agreed moving in the day after completion was a very good idea.

Thursday, 12th March 2020

Just returned home from moving an elderly man into his new retirement home over the last two days, his main concern was fitting an old dining table into the new flat; he had to take a window out from his old house to remove it and then we had to dismantle it before it would fit in his new home…

I have switched on the news for the update on Covid19 Coronavirus to hear Boris Johnson announcing:

'Some of us will lose loved ones before their time.'

The next day, stock markets go in to free fall, the death toll starts to rise and there is not a toilet roll to be had anywhere.

Friday, 20th March 2020

Nobody is moving home; chancellor, Rishi Sunak, says the government will pay 80% of worker's salaries under a new furlough scheme; Boris closes all pubs, restaurants, gyms and schools. It is apparent he will be locking the country down soon so I phone the customer I am moving next Friday to suggest they bring their moving day forward if possible.

Wednesday, 25th March 2020

Boris Johnson did announce a lockdown of the country on Monday evening which will be ratified by parliament this Thursday; we have therefore loaded this lady's belongings yesterday and are delivering them to a self-storage unit in Nottingham today.

I feel slightly vindicated when driving on a deserted M1 motorway as our customer is a hospital worker trying to return to her parent's home. She will be working in her local hospital and storing the furniture in a metal storage container which is attached to a farm in the middle of nowhere.

You would have thought that we could not self-isolate more if we tried but as we are unloading, a local couple arrive to remove some personal items from the storage container next to our customers. The virus has not really affected the people in this part of the country yet as it has in Harrow with 21 dying in Northwick Park hospital alone over the last weekend, so when they hear that we are from London, they cannot leave quick enough.

The news that Boris Johnson has now tested positive for Coronavirus makes it seem more real; this will be our last job for some time as we can no longer safely visit customer's homes to carry out their removal and still keep our distance.